In
The
~~Line~~
of Duty

Lewis Rigler,
Texas Ranger,
Retired

"A Texas Ranger could ride like a Mexican,
trail like an Indian, shoot like a Tennessean,
and fight like the devil."
—Unattributed popular saying

"The Texas Rangers are what they are
because their enemies have been what they were.
The Rangers had to be superior to survive.
Their enemies were pretty good . . .
[the Rangers] had to be better."
—Walter Prescott Webb

IN
THE
LINE
OF DUTY

Reflections of a Texas Ranger Private

Lewis C. Rigler and Judyth W. Rigler

Afterword by Erik T. Rigler

University of North Texas Press
Denton, Texas

Second Edition first printed 1995
with a new afterword by Erik T. Rigler

10 9 8 7 6 5 4 3 2 1

Requests for permission to reproduce material from this work should be
sent to

Permissions
University of North Texas Press
Post Office Box 13856
Denton, Texas 76203

The paper used in this book meets the minimum requirements of the
American National Standard for Permanence of Paper for Printed Library
materials, Z39.48.1984. Binding materials have been chosen for durability.

Library of Congress Cataloging-in-Publication Data

Rigler, Lewis C., 1914–
In the line of duty: reflections of a Texas Ranger private / by Lewis
C. Rigler and Judyth Wagner Rigler. — [Rev. and updated ed.]
p.   cm.
ISBN 0-929398-99-8

1. Rigler, Lewis C., 1914–   . 2. Texas Rangers—Biography.
I. Rigler, Judyth Wagner. II. Title.
HV7911.R53A34 1995
363.2'092—dc20
[B]   95–16646
CIP

DEDICATION

This book is dedicated to the memory of
G. W. "Woody" Blanton, Sheriff of Grayson County
for twenty-three years.
He was co-worker, counselor, and friend—
a man who was everything a partner in the field of law
enforcement should be.

CONTENTS

FOREWORD

Many years ago, I began the speaking engagements that were to become perhaps the most enjoyable of all my Ranger duties. From the beginning, I loved sharing my ideas and opinions with an audience, and soon I found myself in demand for speeches to groups all over Texas and in Louisiana, Oklahoma and Arkansas. I developed quite a good feeling about it and began to agree with the people who praised my efforts—I was pretty smart, and what I had to say was surely important!

One day in the 1950s, I gave a talk in my home town of Gainesville in which I commented on the recent Supreme Court ruling on school integration. While I did not find fault with the justices' opinion, I did say that I thought black children would be at a disadvantage if placed immediately into classes with white children.

At that time, I had an office at the Turner Hotel in Gainesville, and I parked my car on their parking lot. The Turner had a very fine coffee shop in which I spent some time almost every day. All of the kitchen employees were black, and I considered them friends, talking with them often.

After that speech, certain portions of the text were printed in the local paper, including the remark about the black children. About two days later, after working for a few hours in my office, I went down to the parking lot to get in my car and drive home. Stuck under the windshield wiper I found a crudely printed note that read: "Mr. Rigley (sic), who give a dam what you think?!"

What a great message that was—it succeeded in bringing me down a peg or two!

When I decided to write this book, my chief goal was to record my career for the benefit of my children and grandchildren. Many of my family and friends have told me that I have wonderful stories that should be recorded, but I realize that they may be slightly prejudiced. So if you, dear reader, find something here that you consider offensive or that you simply don't agree with, remember that long ago I had to accept the fact that some people don't give a damn what I think!

⋆ ⋆ ⋆

I began my career in law enforcement in 1941, when I entered the Department of Public Safety following two months of training. How has the field changed in that time? In almost every way you could name. But one of the most dramatic developments has been the increase in narcotics use and the problems it has created for law enforcement.

In my first five years as a DPS patrolman, I made only three arrests dealing with narcotics—one was a doctor, one a nurse and one a safe burglar. I never saw or smelled marijuana. I first became aware of the use of marijuana in 1948 or 1949, and it seemed to become more of a problem when servicemen began returning from Korea. That surprised me, because during my Army years, the only drug I ever saw used was beer. There were probably 10,000 soldiers at San Antonio's Fort Sam Houston when I was there, and I knew of no one who used narcotics of any kind.

From the start of our problems with the narcotics explosion, every mistake possible has been made, and we don't seem to have learned anything after all these years about how to control it.

I remember when the Dallas District Attorney's office convicted the notorious stripper Candy Barr of possession of marijuana and gave her fifteen years in the Texas Department of Corrections. This only seemed to give marijuana a big advertising boost.

How can you control the production and use of marijuana

when it grows wild in most of the southern part of the United States? There are even plants growing along major highways where people have thrown out marijuana to avoid having it found on them during a search.

When marijuana use began to increase, it was news when someone was arrested for possession or sale of a very small amount of marijuana. Then it became news only when it involved ten pounds, then a trailer load, a boatload or an airplane load. The publicity is gone—we have flashier and more dangerous drugs to worry about—but the problem still exists.

When the Department of Public Safety first got into the narcotics law enforcement business in the early 1950s, they were hiring highway patrolmen and others with only two years of law enforcement experience as narcotics people. Many were used as underground people to infiltrate the narcotics world. They were given nice, souped-up cars and almost unlimited expense money. For people who are used to earning very little and living from paycheck to paycheck, this seemed like a great life; some even switched sides, becoming users and dealers. We did not have a clue then as to what to do about narcotics, and we still don't.

In 1983, I started a business, Rigler & Rickert Inc., operating as Able Bail Bond Service, with Carl F. Rickert, a former Texas Highway patrolman. In our first eleven years of business, we made 5,500 bail bonds in Cooke County, about 500 in other counties. Many of these bonds are for narcotics violations. Bonds for charges on less than two ounces of marijuana have dropped from $1,000 to $200, and even though we make money from these bails, it would be much better if the offenders were simply given a summons. I don't think they pose nearly the danger to others that driving a car at ninety-miles per hour does.

Cocaine has long been known in the United States as a drug used mostly by the well-to-do. However, the well-to-do smartened up, and someone discovered they could get even richer by making crack or rock cocaine for the poor and ignorant. This has taken over as the drug of choice. Once a person is addicted to crack, there is no cure; while the user may get "clean," the figures aren't encouraging, with many of them getting back on cocaine.

I have been told that addiction to cocaine is very similar to nicotine addiction. That makes it easier for me to understand. I stopped smoking on my twenty-first birthday, after having had the habit for five years. Fourteen years later, I started smoking again and stopped twenty-five years later on my sixtieth birthday. Now at the ripe old age of eighty, I find that I still crave nicotine, but I am too stubborn to smoke again.

Now in order to feed their habits, we have addicts killing convenience store clerks during the course of a ten dollar to twenty dollar armed robbery. There are thefts of all kinds, carjacking, prostitution, and the result is that narcotic use is filling our jails and bankrupting our country.

When we put misdemeanor offenders in jail, we have only put them in an environment where they learn how to be better criminals. Our jails are running over; our prisons are not accepting any more prisoners. I believe that if you put a person in jail often enough, he or she will get to where they like it.

As a young man I joined the Army, and for nine or ten months, I really was unhappy. Slowly, I came to like being told when to get up, when to go to bed, when to eat, what to wear; and if I had not married, I would have re-enlisted. Prisoners now being held in county jails anxiously await their transfer to the Texas State prison. Why? More freedom, more schooling, and possibly a better chance to obtain drugs.

So we have, as the saying goes, met the enemy; what are we to do about it? Surely, the federal government will only continue to throw money at it. Try as they will, they can do little more than keep fine records of the small amounts of drugs and cash seized, the arrests and the convictions. But the sale and use go on.

As radical as it sounds, I would propose to legalize what you could of the drug trade and use the money for something worthwhile such as a national health plan. Take the profit out of dealing in drugs, and the demand will go down.

The one thing that does seem to work is education, starting at the grade school level. I know from observation of some thirty years that you can't cure two percent of cocaine and heroin addicts. Their use of the drug and their dirty needles have spread AIDS all over our land.

When I came to Cooke County in 1947, the bootleggers were really doing well; they were thriving also in Denton County, Grayson, Collin, Montague and others. The liquor interest controlled much of Oklahoma; I did not go to many Oklahoma counties unless I made arrangements with a member of the Oklahoma Crime Bureau to meet me; doing any less was foolhardy.

With parts of Cooke County now wet, there is no use for a bootlegger. It is my belief that less whiskey is consumed per person now than when the county was dry, but beer and wine are the alcoholic drinks of choice with most people. Liquor as we know it is a drug. As I sit with a can of light beer after mowing the grass on a hot day, I can't visualize it as a drug, but there you are.

Some things from my growing-up years on a farm outside Lorena, Texas, stand out clearly in my mind. I remember when the Volstead Act became law. No more whiskey, beer, wine or any kind of alcohol could be legally sold. Did it succeed? For sure it did not. It only produced bad alcoholic drinks, bad people and lots of hypocrites.

The difference between alcohol then and such drugs as cocaine and marijuana now is that the great majority of the law-abiding citizens did not want prohibition to succeed. What was the great attraction of alcohol? The fact that it was illegal made people suddenly want it even more. Before long, there was ample bootlegging to supply everyone's needs.

I well remember a German family who lived adjacent to our farm. They were good farmers, but they began making bootleg whiskey. Soon cars were coming to their farm at all hours, going up the lane by our place. When it rained, the road would get very muddy, and my uncle would charge five dollars to get a team of mules to pull the stuck cars out of the mud. We all liked the rain, because it increased our income. Later the German family lost everything trying to stay out of the federal penitentiary. They did very little time but spent up all their wealth on legal costs.

Another big change in law enforcement since my days is the so-called "quota system" that places demands on all agencies to include in their ranks people of both sexes and all ethnicities. In the February 1994 issue of *Texas Monthly*, Robert Draper wrote an article entitled "The Myth of the Texas Ranger." In this article, much is made of the hiring of two females who many have argued were not qualified to be peace officers on the level of the Rangers. In fact, longtime Ranger Joaquin Jackson, the model for the role Nick Nolte played in "Extreme Prejudice," is quoted as saying he retired because these women were hired.

This story is just a blip on the history of hiring practices at the DPS, federal and municipal agencies. The famed quota system is in place: we will hire so many blacks, so many Hispanics, so many Asians and so many females. Forget about where each finished in a competition; just give me the ones to fill the quota.

But on the issue of women in the Rangers, I am sure to be outvoted. My wife, five daughters, three daughters-in-law and eleven granddaughters would certainly have a say on any opinion I express in this regard, but I believe that each agency suffers and the public suffers because of this kind of mandated hiring.

This is not to say that hiring practices were not faulty or subject to abuse in the past. As an example, some thirty-five years ago a high-ranking member of the state legislature approached Col. Homer Garrison and asked that a former sheriff from his area, who had been defeated in his re-election bid, be made a Ranger. Garrison told him he had fifty-one Rangers and no vacancies. The legislator countered, "If you had a vacancy, would you take him based on his character and ability?" Garrison said he would surely consider it. Guess what? At the next meeting of the Texas Legislature, the Ranger force was increased by one. The man was appointed; he was a fine man and had a good career with the Rangers. I worked with him many days at the infamous 1968 and 1969 Lone Star Steel strike, and he was a good worker and a pleasant companion. But he shouldn't have been hired in the way that he was.

I have seen Ranger captains who had no experience at a supervisory level be put in charge by the state governor. Not every governor, certainly, but I will say that Governor Coke Stevenson did get such a man made a Ranger, and later a captain, and the appointee moved the headquarters to a small town and was an embarrassment to all Rangers.

The old way of getting into the Rangers might not have been totally fair, but it was very successful. The Rangers were constantly looking at the working abilities of sheriffs, Texas highway patrolmen and other officers. They wanted a top-notch performer. When Col. Jim Adams was head of DPS, he passed a rule that only members of the Department of Public Safety could become Rangers, and this seemed unfair.

Not all Rangers were perfect; not all Rangers were good; but overall, they did an outstanding job. I never knew of a Ranger being convicted of a felony. Most were good family men, strong leaders in their communities, and excellent role models.

Throughout my life, I have always been aware of how driven our culture is by myths and half-truths, hero worship and all kinds of misplaced loyalties. The Texas A&M tradition of the 12th man is now more than seventy-five years old, but how many know that the twelfth man never entered the game? Look at the sterling image of the Royal Canadian Mounted Police; who knows what made them famous? The late movie hero John Wayne never was in a war—but try telling that to those rabid fans who still consider him the greatest American hero ever born.

I was in a major department store in Denton County recently and saw a member of the Dallas Cowboys, a defensive back, signing autographs; the line of people stretched all over the store. Outside of a few flashy moves on the football field, this man has no history; we know almost nothing about him. People are just searching for heroes today.

Another change made in the Ranger service since my retirement in 1977 is that there are no more Ranger privates. The Ranger private was a unique character; he just wanted to work, and the number of hours spent on a case meant nothing. Now they tell me that a Ranger can work only a certain number of hours per week without calling for permission and then drawing overtime. I think, how sad. Criminals do not do their crimes for the benefit of officers on a time schedule.

The Ranger private was loyal to the captain as long as the captain was loyal to him. Captains M.T. Gonzaullas, Bob Crowder, E.G. Banks and Bill Wilson knew what a captain was and what his place in the Rangers was. They were capable and good people, and all of them had been good privates as well. Now they make a man a Ranger and the next second he is a sergeant. Maybe they know what they're doing, but it was always my experience that a criminal responded better to a private than to someone with rank.

For me and many of my friends, being a Texas Ranger was something like being in the promised land. Always, each day, there was a challenge—safe burglaries, bank robberies, cattle thefts, murders, assaults, strikes where violence occurred, kidnapping, forgery, con games, going to court. We did love it—working with fellow Rangers who were trusted and good friends, having a family of contemporaries you could depend on, being needed in different counties, being free to do a criminal investigation in your own way, even the association with some thieves and robbers, who in many ways had good qualities. Information I got from some of them saved my life two or three times, and helped me solve cases. I would not and could not do it again. Times change. The way it was is not the way it is now; the song is gone but the memory lingers on.

I often think of the time when my son, Rick, got out of the service, finished his master's degree, and wanted to become a police officer. I would have been happy for him to have come into the DPS and possibly to the Ranger service, but that can sometimes result in unfair comparisons. When Rick went into the FBI, I was satisfied. I believe his starting pay in 1971 was twice what I was making, and the last year I worked, 1976 to 1977, I made $16,000.

The pay of a Ranger in 1946 was $175 per month; for sergeants, $200; captains, $250. By 1957, Ranger privates made about $410. Not until 1947 did the DPS have any health or retirement benefits for its officers. The agency paid for none of the moves Rangers had to make; when we moved from Grand Prairie to Gainesville I borrowed a stake-bedded truck and we moved all of our belongings in one trip. Our expense accounts would never cover a hotel stay if we were on the road; sometimes we slept in jury rooms or a fire station. Yet we considered ourselves lucky, and I wouldn't change a thing about those years.

✫ ✫ ✫

How do you say "so long" to a book that has been developing since you were six years old? Well, you say thanks. Thanks to my family, to my friends, to my teachers, and my church in my formative years in the little town of Lorena, Texas.

Thanks to my country for having the Civilian Conservation Corps when I and countless thousands of others needed it most. Thanks to the Army for teaching me discipline and the ability to get along with others.

Thanks to the judges and the lawyers—on both sides—and to the sheriffs and the chiefs of police. Thanks to the government agencies such as the FBI and Secret Service. Thanks to all the officers I met in Texas and other states. Thanks to my comrades in the Department of Public Safety—with a special thanks to the late Col. Homer Garrison Jr., who inspired me in so many ways.

Thanks to the vast majority of Texas citizens, who over the years have supported the Rangers and other law enforcement groups. Thanks to the city of Waco and everyone who has made the Col. Homer Garrison Memorial Museum and the Ranger Hall of Fame a continuing success.

Thanks to my late wife, Leah, and our three sons, Steve, Mike, Rick, who took me part of the way. Thanks to Joyce and our five daughters, Lynda, Charlotte, Patti, Diane, Jan, now grown women, and the same three boys, now men, who together still guide my life and make it a pleasure. And thanks to my daughter-in-law Judyth, who has worked with me on this book, and to my other in-laws, who must get very tired of hearing about what the

Ranger has done and is going to do. You have always had the goodhearted spirit to applaud my efforts, and I appreciate it.

Note: Although eleven years have passed since the first publication of this book, it was decided that the narrative should remain as it was written in 1984. Only a few corrections have been made to the original text.

Lewis Rigler's Family
From left to right, first row: Joyce & Lewis Rigler
Second row: Diane, Patti, Lynda
Third row: Steve, Charlotte, Jan, Mike
Fourth row: Erik

White Robes and Torches

Cotton. They called it "King Cotton," and only those who knew of the plant firsthand were able fully to understand the title of respect so grudgingly given it. While it grew, from the first tiny sprout shouldering its way up through soft spring earth to the last bristly, sticky boll harvested in the dry, cracked field under a relentless sun, cotton was king. It ruled over its kingdom with extreme cruelty, turning all who waited upon it into slaves.

There was no joy in serving this tough master, only pain of body and spirit. Harvesting cotton was a nightmare—the workers' hands remained sore and red for days after picking. Those who endured bent backs and torn hands in the oppressive summer heat of Central Texas felt that cotton was the meanest growing thing alive.

One of my earliest memories is of bending over the spiteful plants in the heat, dragging behind me what seemed a bottomless ducking sack much larger than I. Only six, I had been living and working on a farm outside Lorena, Texas, near Waco, for almost a year. The previous year, 1920, our family had come upon hard times, and my father, mother, two sisters, brother, and I had moved from our own farm into Lorena. A short time after that move, my father, John William Rigler, contracted typhoid fever while on a hay baling job and died at the age of forty. The family then moved in with my maternal grandmother, Mrs. Thomas Alfred Linville; however, I very soon was much of the time on the Linville farm with my Uncle George Linville and his family, working to earn my keep.

Uncle George worked harder than anyone I've ever known and expected me to do likewise. I could milk a cow as well as anyone by the time I was eight years old, and I learned to plow with horses and mules at about the same age. Uncle George didn't own a tractor until many more years later. I cannot remember a single time when there wasn't any work to do.

There was not much I was sure of at that early age, but one thing I did know for certain—I did *not* want to be a farmer. Like all young boys, I imagined an exciting, perhaps dangerous, life for myself. The events in Lorena during that summer and fall of 1921 certainly provided fuel for the fire of my already-active imagination.

In the post-World War I fever of patriotism, many causes, some less than honorable, appeared or reappeared on the scene. One of these was the Ku Klux Klan, which suddenly seemed to be undergoing a revival right under our noses. Everywhere I looked, the letters "KKK" were painted. Bonfires blazed on the hills outside of town all that summer, and the grapevine buzzed with rumors of the Klan's activities, viewed with a mixture of curiosity and fear by most.

It is difficult now to imagine the appeal of such a cruelly destructive group. But even the fraternal lodges and churches were attracted at first, for the Klan was shrewd enough to call upon the people's belief in God, the protection of womanhood, and allegiance to country. But I also remember hearing early on that if you were a Catholic, a Jew, a black, or a Republican, the Klan was not for you.

As the summer heat dragged on into fall, rumors about the Klan's activities became more and more frequent, and many people were genuinely frightened. Often, people kept the lights in their homes burning all night. Those not in the Klan never answered the door without a shotgun handy.

One day we heard that the Klan was planning a giant parade for Lorena the first of October. Why the little town of Lorena was chosen, I still do not know, but everyone was very excited. The parade was set to start shortly after dark, and I was to be allowed to watch from my grandmother's house, which was just one block south of the main street. Imagine my excitement—at last I would get to see the previously invisible Klan!

People came from everywhere for the big event. Lorena was overrun with people on foot, and others on horseback, in cars, wagons, buggies and surreys. Most of the farmers who lived outside of town came in that day. I can still recall being fascinated by the patch of white skin on each farmer's brow that was exposed when he would remove his hat, which he seldom was without, to wipe away the sweat. The women were dressed plainly in faded dresses they'd made from low-cost fabrics. The parade afforded free amusement, and very few would dare to miss it. The water in Lorena was turned off about 2:00 P.M. If you wanted liquid refreshment, the soda water concessions were ready to serve you, for a fee! The popcorn salesman on the corner charged five cents for a large bag of the salty stuff and made sixty-five dollars that day.

The parade plan was for half of the Klansmen to start one mile south of town and half of them one mile north of town. They would meet at the street which ran west through the business section, continue across the Katy tracks, and march through the Negro area. About 4:30 P.M. word was passed through the crowd that Sheriff Buchanan of Waco, Chief Deputy Red Burton and Deputy Mack Wood were in Lorena and had met with Klan leaders and told them that if they were going to have the parade, they could not wear masks over their faces. Truths, half-truths and rumors spread quickly. First, we heard that the parade had been called off, then that it was back on, then that the Klan would consent to taking off their masks, then that they wouldn't. It was a busy afternoon for gossip.

At one point during that hot afternoon, the Baptist and Methodist preachers got together and talked with the sheriff and his deputies and then with the leaders of the Klan, trying to stop the parade that they knew could end in violence. The Klan was determined to march, though, and the lawmen were equally determined to maintain order. There was just bound to be trouble.

Finally, the long-awaited event got under way. The night was warm and humid. Since Lorena at that time had only one or two street lamps, torches were used to light the area. The light from those flames upon the darkness of the street, upon the faces of the townspeople and, later, upon the white uniforms and masks created quite an eerie scene. I can to this day see it all clearly in my mind.

I wandered away from the house to get closer to the action, in with the crowd surging toward the main street. As a small boy, of course, I had trouble seeing anything more than the overalls of the farmers around me. Then I moved away, off by myself, to get a better view. When the parade members coming from the north got to within sixty to eighty yards of the main street, Buchanan, Burton and Wood stopped the leader on horseback because the marchers, some one hundred of them, were masked. I could hear shouting from both sides but had trouble making out what was being said.

Suddenly everything changed. Within seconds of the meeting in the street between the marchers and the law, a shooting and "cutting" spree had broken out. Horses, spooked by the sudden noise of the violence, broke and ran in all directions. People were screaming and running everywhere. I can remember just standing with my mouth open, taking it all in. A man whose name I remember as Louis Crow, who ran a laundry in Waco, was fatally injured early in the fight; his body somehow remained on his horse until the horse reached the railroad tracks, where the body fell to the ground. His macabre ride was a frightening experience for many of those who saw him. Sheriff Buchanan was shot, and Deputy Burton helped him into a drug store run by a Catholic at one corner of the main street. Burton locked the doors after them and somehow stood off the crowd which was pushing to get inside, both for fear of staying outside amid the violence, and out of curiosity about what was happening inside.

My uncle, Winfield F. Linville, was working in the store and was witness to all that went on inside. An ambulance from Waco was summoned and finally arrived. Buchanan was taken out through a loading chute in the back of Evans and Westbrook Mercantile Store, which was connected to the drug store. It was thought that the Klan had the road to the north blocked, so the ambulance went west and through the country to McGregor and then on to Waco, a distance of some thirty-five to forty miles, rather than taking the fourteen-mile direct route. It was a miracle that the sheriff survived the trip.

The others who had been hurt were taken into the Mercantile Store, where bolts of fabric were hung across the windows to provide some privacy and protection for the wounded.

Most of those in the parade, surprised and frightened at the sudden eruption of violence, removed their robes and quietly returned to their homes, some in Lorena, others farther away. No one, except for the leaders and the lawmen, had anticipated the violence, and many had been taken in and then were ashamed of their part in it.

Spectators broke into small groups and dispersed after first comparing versions of the afternoon and evening's excitement, which would form the fabric of colorful stories for years to come. By morning all was quiet in Lorena again.

For a time, the Klan issue remained a controversial one. A series of fires occurred in the days following the march; these were blamed on the Klan. "These fires are getting to be a regular hyperdermic" was the slightly off-base comment of one man, a railroad foreman named Junior, upon viewing yet another blaze.

There was no neutral ground on this issue; you were either Klan or anti-Klan. Governor Pat M. Neff of Waco decided that the group should not be allowed to terrorize the state any longer, and he rallied the help of other anti-Klansmen and law enforcement officers. The Klan fell apart and had no strength of note in Texas after that.

Sheriff Buchanan, something of a hero, recovered, but he was defeated when he ran for re-election. Red Burton later became a Texas Ranger, serving with distinction. Then he was chief of detectives and, finally, chief of police with the City of Waco. We became friends in the early 1950s. I was with Red many times, but I never mentioned this affair to him nor he to me, though he knew through our mutual friend, retired Ranger Captain Tom Hickman, that I was at that parade as a young boy. It was part of an unwritten understanding among law officers to avoid subjects like this one, still marked by grief and hard feelings in spite of the years that had passed. Red was killed in an automobile accident near Waco when he was in his eighties. In my opinion, he was one top gentleman, as well as a fine lawman.

It seems to me now as I look back on that incident that I had no doubt of the courage, the right, and the duty of those three officers to uphold the law against great odds. I guess that hot, violent night was when I first had the feeling that someday I would be an officer of the law. I have been in many places and seen many things since that October of 1921, but nothing has come close to that scene for its reality and drama.

2

Horseback to Helicopters

According to the U. S. Census Bureau's 1980 figures, there are 14,228,383 Texans. About ninety of them are Texas Rangers. The Ranger force has changed greatly in organization and policy to meet ever-changing needs over the years, although its span of service has not been entirely continuous. Still, the Texas Rangers have been around almost without interruption since colonization days.

The Rangers were first established in 1823 as a loosely organized group of some ten men hired by Stephen F. Austin to protect the early Texas settlers from the attacks of the Indians trying to regain their lost land, and from the Mexican bandits who were crossing the Rio Grande River into Texas to rob and pillage. Since each man was required to range over a wide area to scout for marauding Indians, the force became known as "Rangers."

The Permanent Council of the Texas Revolution authorized the recruiting of twenty-five volunteer Rangers on November 1, 1835. Later the group was enlarged to 150 men, and Ranger service became a paid position. Enlistment was for one year, and the salary of the Ranger in those days was rations, clothing, horse service, and one dollar and thirty-five cents per day.

The authority of the Ranger in those days was virtually unlimited, but his qualifications were, at best, questionable. Physical strength far outweighed formal schooling as a prerequisite for the job; as a result, most were under twenty-one years of age, and very few were educated. Not one was ordinary.

It has been said that reports were particularly bothersome for the early Rangers, some of whom could barely write. One Ranger reported to his captain after a battle with bootleggers on the border:

> The other day we run on to some horsebackers on our side of the border and one of them thought he would learn me how to shoot, so I naturalized him—made an American citizen out of him.

Another early Ranger is alleged to have avoided a troublesome (and potentially damaging) report by turning in this brief, but to the point, message:

> Crime . . . . Cattle Theft
> Defendant . . . . . Ollie Peterson
> Disposition . . . . Damn bad—had to kill him

What those first Rangers lacked in education and manners, they compensated for in unswerving determination and dedication to their jobs. Possibly the most famous anecdote testifying to their strength and toughness was popularized when a prizefight scheduled in Dallas in 1896 was cancelled due to a local ruling. The people were so incensed that they began rioting, and city officials put out an urgent call for Ranger assistance. The story goes that city officials gathered at the depot to meet the train and were aghast when a single Ranger, Captain Bill McDonald, stepped off. They demanded to know why more men had not been sent. The terse reply was, "You ain't got but one riot, have you?" This line gave birth to the "One Riot, One Ranger" motto that adorns several Ranger statues and is the most frequently told Ranger anecdote.

Another tribute to the toughness of the Rangers is credited to a U. S. Army officer who witnessed a single Ranger quell and disarm an insurgent band of twenty men. The witness later said, "A Ranger would charge Hell with a bucket of water." About the same time, another anecdote was popularized by a frontier official who came upon a couple of Rangers surrounded by the bodies of many slain bandits. When asked what had happened, one of the Rangers is said to have drawled, "We had a little shooting match—and they lost." I have often wished for a return to this terseness of reporting.

The Ranger's primary duty in the early days was to protect the Texas settler from the Indian and later the Mexican bandit, and occasionally from both. The Indian was not normally a teammate of the Mexican but did share a common goal—to eliminate the white intruder. Eventually the Indian realized the fierceness of the Texas-Mexican struggle and retreated to await the outcome.

The original area the Ranger served was quite small but was gradually expanded with the Texas Frontier. The Ranger met the need and was not bound to county borders but could move as one man or as thirty. He was independent of local voters and influences, and effective in organized counties where the supremacy of the law was threatened. One Ranger could make an arrest, escort prisoners, and guard jails; he could suppress a riot or strengthen the back of a wavering judge or sheriff. If more Rangers were required, word was sent.

During the late 1840s the Rangers participated in the Mexican War with General Zachary Taylor. It was here that the Rangers became nationally known. They stood apart from the regular Army, with their long beards and mustaches and wide variety of garments. A rougher group was never seen. Among them at that time, surprisingly, were many college graduates, doctors, and lawyers. The adventure of service was what drew these men into the Rangers.

During the Civil War, the Ranger organization was neglected. Many Rangers and former Rangers enlisted in "Terry's Texas Rangers," a Confederate unit commanded by Colonel Benjamin Franklin Terry. They were reorganized during the Reconstruction period by Governor E. J. Davis and were used to enforce carpetbagger laws, unpopular with many Texas citizens. They were disbanded with the overthrow of the Reconstruction government.

In 1874, the Rangers were reorganized as two units—the Special Force of Rangers, whose job was to put down banditry along the Rio Grande, and the Frontier Battalion, made up of mobile companies sent wherever they were needed. During this time, they were employed in the famous Salt War, as well as in the killing of Sam Bass and members of his famous robber band. Salaries in those days ranged from forty dollars per month for privates to seventy-five dollars per month for lieutenants. A widely syndicated newspaper featured an article stating that one Ranger captain enlisted only teetotalers who were church members and nonsmokers. Not all of the captains were this strict, but the Ranger was required to have a reputation beyond reproach and be polite and gentlemanly at all times. This requirement did not mean that injustices were not done to men; during this period, "Moonlight Extraditions" became common, as Rangers kidnapped Mexican prisoners and brought them to Texas for punishment. Here began the Ranger-Mexican battle which continues today, and here the tales of Ranger brutality toward Mexicans got their start.

In June 1900, the Ranger force was reduced to four companies of six men each through a ruling by the state's attorney general on the 1874 law originally authorizing the Rangers. Over a year later, legislation was enacted increasing the size of the force, primarily used for West Texas and the Mexican border. Historian Walter Prescott Webb said that four horses existed for the Ranger during this period: the Revolution within Mexico, Prohibition, World War I, and the Texas Oil Boom. Indeed, he was correct, but perhaps a fifth horse was present: politics.

In the early 1900s, unethical practices stemming from the increase in the number of Rangers caused them to fall into disfavor. A period of poor government in Texas fostered a spoils system that resulted in the Ranger force's growth from 150 to 1,000 members. Badges were handed out recklessly, and the result was a disaster. Many of the appointees used their badges to win special favors or to intimidate others. By 1920, many Texans were calling for abolishment of the Ranger force.

In 1935 a new governor, James V. Allred, set in motion an upheaval and overhaul of the Ranger force. Allred appointed Albert S. Johnson to serve as chairman of the newly created Public Safety Commission. Johnson's first duty was to stop the distribution of honorary badges and to begin calling in those given out over the years, some 3,000. He relocated the Rangers to a site in north Austin, where they became a part of the Department of Public Safety along with the Texas Highway Patrol, License and Weight Division, and headquarters personnel. Higher standards were set for Rangers. Hundreds were fired, and the remainder were completely retrained. Political pull as a means to appointment to Ranger service was replaced by examination and recommendation. Performance and seniority were considered before any Ranger was promoted. To be considered, an applicant had to be between thirty and forty-five years old, at least five feet eight inches tall, and of sound mind and body. Each man received training in techniques of fingerprinting, communications, ballistics, and recordkeeping.

The Rangers now operated with a group of forty privates, six sergeants, and six captains distributed among the companies. But even with the department's overhaul and higher standards, the Ranger found himself in the news time and time again. Politics, strikes, race relations, and other controversial cases have contributed to the Ranger force's being the brunt of various forms of disfavor through the years. Yet the Ranger endures as Texas' oldest law enforcement officer.

The modern Ranger presents a sharp contrast with the early swashbuckling image of a man in Western twill, Stetson hat, and boots, riding horseback across the prairie in pursuit of a retreating bandit. Some still wear Western-cut business suits and boots, but the horse has been replaced, for the most part, by state cars and helicopters.

Communications have come a long way in their application to Ranger work since the early days. In the 1870s, 1880s, and 1890s, one aid to Rangers was the *List of Fugitives from Justice,* a listing of people wanted by the authorities for assorted criminal acts, compiled by the State of Texas Adjutant General's office from reports submitted by county sheriffs across the state. Rangers carried this and studied it with such fervor (partly because of the rewards posted on the heads of wanted men) that it was nicknamed "Bible II" or "The Crime Book." Along with the name of the wanted man appeared a description—approximate age, height, weight, and color of hair and eyes—and supplemental, often colorful information like this: "Moore, George—has sister in Houston known as Dancing Eliza; Smith, Fred—heavy growth of hair on hands; Rose, J. D.—broken knife blade in right shoulder."

In the early 1900s, communications in law enforcement continued to make advances. Lee Simmons, Sheriff of Grayson County about 1912, and later head of the Texas Prison System,

Four Ranger Captains, from left to right: Tom Hickman, M. T. Gonzaullas, Bob Crowder, and Clint Peoples, ca. 1958 in Austin, Texas.

told me once about methods in those days. If an officer needed to catch someone who had fled his county, penny postcards were used. A description of the charges against a wanted man was written on the card and sent to sheriffs, chiefs of police, constables, and city marshals. Surprisingly, this system worked very well, he said, for the population of Texas was not great and people were not mobile as they are now.

By the time I went to work, radio communications had arrived, but they were in the infancy of their utilization by law enforcement agencies. None of the Texas Highway Patrol motorcycles had radios. As early as 1938 or 1939, some of the DPS cars were equipped with receivers. In 1941, the DPS had a radio transmitter at the Ranger Station in Fair Park. It transmitted on AM 1658, and the Dallas police transmitted on AM 1714. The first patrol car we had, a 1941 Ford, had a receiver. If you did not respond to a call, then service stations along the road you worked were notified, and they hung out a white cloth. I remember so well the first two-way radio-equipped car we had, a 1942 Ford. The transmitter required about an eight-foot cane pole wrapped tightly with copper wire. If you broke the pole, you were in trouble. Seeing a highway patrol car going down the street where there were trees, you'd think a drunk was driving. Due to the limited distance we could successfully transmit, in outlying areas we ran a copper wire antenna to the top of the municipal water tank; then if we had to call in, we tied the transmitter to this device.

The Dallas transmitters in the early forties operated from 8:00 A.M. to midnight, except Friday and Saturday, when they stayed on until 2:00 A.M. I recall one morning when my partner, Royce Calvert, and I were driving into Oak Cliff from Grand Prairie. We were stopped by another motorist who informed us of a bad wreck north of Waxahachie on Highway 77. We called the radio station to get ambulances and other officers to the scene, and the operator was not answering—finally, a voice came on that belonged to our janitor, and all he said was, "Three nine nine, there ain't nobody here." The accident involved a flatbed truck loaded with workers and a gasoline transport, and I believe seventeen people were killed. Perhaps some could have been saved if we had been able to get help. Advancements in communications have done much for law enforcement since those days.

The average Ranger of today is about forty-five years old and brings about twelve years of law enforcement experience to his appointment. Most come from the ranks of the state troopers. Three-fourths of the members are over six feet tall, but the original height requirement has been relaxed somewhat; a few Rangers still boast that they are on the force pending several inches' growth in height, and I was one of these. Most Rangers are from rural areas. Over half have had some college, and this is increasing yearly as older Rangers retire, and are replaced by younger, better-educated men.

The duties of the Rangers have changed a great deal over the years, but the Ranger is still charged, as he was then, with four basic duties:

1. Protection of life and property through enforcement of the criminal statutes of the state of Texas.
2. The suppression of riots and insurrections.
3. The investigation of major crimes, such as murder, rape, robbery, burglary, cattle theft, felonious assault, and other felonies.
4. The apprehension of fugitives. In this connection Rangers transport prisoners and assist local prosecutors in compiling information for court action.

Rangers often work disaster areas following hurricanes, tornadoes, or explosions. One or more Rangers are assigned to the governor as guard each time he/she is out of Austin. Rangers are also assigned to visiting politicians, dignitaries, and the like. Emphasis is placed on cooperating with local police officers in investigating major crimes; Rangers are called in as needed and work side by side with local peace officers. As Texas is divided into six districts encompassing 254 counties and some 267,000 square miles, the Ranger still "ranges" over a wide area. His car is really his office. The Ranger also frequently speaks at business and social functions as an ambassador to the public and an emblem of Texas tradition.

About once a year, some political hopeful invariably speaks out for abolishment of the Texas Rangers on the grounds that their job is obsolete. Quick and loud rebuttal from Ranger supporters follows, a week or so of controversy ensues, and finally the conflict dies down for another year or two. With more than a century and a half of service, it seems unlikely that the Texas Rangers will be allowed to fade from our state's law enforcement organization. The Texas Rangers continue to accomplish their tasks, routine and unusual, with efficiency and dedication. The Rangers are both a major force in the constant battle for law and order in our enormous state and perhaps the last remaining link with the colorful history that has made Texas what it is today.

3

Gettin' By

I was born in Waco, Texas, August 7, 1914, to John William Rigler and Sallie Linville Rigler. My father's people came to this country from Germany, my mother's from Scotland and Ireland. For a time my people were dairy farmers.

As I was growing up on the family farm outside Lorena, I guess I knew we were poor, but I learned early that we could get by with very little. We had a used buggy and a one-eyed gray mare named Nell. We had no electricity, but about fifteen gallons of kerosene would keep the lamps going for a year. Wood was plentiful, and corncobs could also be burned. There was no ice-box; in the summer our food was kept by placing it in a bucket and lowering it into the well or by putting it into what was called a cooler, a metal box with shelves, kept filled with well water absorbed by ducking material on rollers for cooling the food and keeping it moist. Baths were a treat, available only once or twice a week. Many people thought too much bathing could weaken a person. For my father's bath, a No. 3 washtub would be filled and set out in the sun in the morning so the water would be warm at night. In the winter, water was heated for bathing on the wood cookstove.

Lewis as a baby being held on the pony by his mother.

After my father's death in 1920, things were really tough for us. My father had been a day laborer the last year or so of his life, never earning more than three dollars a day for sunup-to-sundown work. He left no insurance money, no bank account, no property.

I can remember very little about my father, since he died when I was barely six. I've been told he had some accounting skill and had taken courses at a Waco business college. He kept books for people for a time. He was also a good carpenter. He liked to read, but he didn't much care for small talk. I can't remember the sound of his voice, but I can remember some things about him: he was a good juggler, and he was a hard worker (he worked forty acres on the halves). I can remember washing the old buggy with him, and I can remember going into Lorena with him in a wagon on a Saturday to take in a bale of cotton. I can remember watching him cut up chewing tobacco for his pipe. I can remember him sending me back to the house to get water when he was picking cotton or working in the field.

My father made a crop on the piece of land he worked in 1919, but then things must have gone bad. He borrowed a wagon and team, loaded up everything we owned, and we all headed into town to live in a rent house in Lorena. I can recall sitting on what was then called a davenport, with my father driving the team and wagon up that hill to town, with the people looking at us and thinking, "Here comes another bunch that couldn't make it on the farm."

And then he was dead. By the time I was not much more than six, I knew I'd been dealt a sort of funny hand in life, and I didn't see any hope of anyone coming to lead me out of the bulrushes. I had no father figure to guide me. My mother went to work at the McClendon and Brown Ice Cream Company in Waco, handwrapping Eskimo Pies in tinfoil for twelve dollars a week. She stayed there in Waco during the week with her sister, and we stayed with Grandmother Linville, who made a valiant effort to cope with the situation. She took in boarders to make a little money, but we were always just one step in front of being broke.

I was farmed out early, spending weekends and the growing season with Uncle George and Aunt Mittie on their dairy farm. Uncle George kept between thirty and forty cows. I have always wondered why people say cows "give" milk—that's just not true, I can tell you. You have to *take* it away from them, and that is truly an art. Morning and evening, two of us would milk hard for two or three hours. Then we would run the crank by hand to separate the cream. After it soured, we'd put it in a barrel churn and churn it until it made butter. Then we'd use a butter paddle to force out the last of the water. The resulting butter was placed in a one-pound mold, removed, and wrapped in waxed paper. We sold the butter on a route in Waco about once a week. Uncle George had an old Model "T" Ford he used for these trips. I can remember many people who lived several miles from town and had to walk home carrying their supplies. We were all so proud of Uncle George when he had "G. D. Linville, Rt. #3, Lorena, Texas" printed on the waxed paper wrapping. We got fifty cents a pound for the butter.

We also raised oats, cotton, corn, and hay on Uncle George's farm. He was a hard worker and a hard man to please. In the fall, he would have us all in the cotton fields before daylight. I have sat at the end of a row many a morning, waiting for it to get light enough to see the cotton. Once we got up at the wrong rooster crowing, about one in the morning, and sat in the field for several hours before we realized what we had done. By then it was too late to go back to bed. That was one long day. I learned early to run a hay press and man a double-disc plow. But the only things I liked about that farm were the cows and the pigs we raised.

Farm life was hard, for sure, but the biggest problem was the loneliness. You just never saw many people. The postman was a very important figure in our lives. If you were out plowing, the post man might stop and tell you some real news—a gin caught on fire in Lorena last night, or Old Lady Barnes was real sick. Radio didn't really hit its heyday in the rural areas until the late 1930s, and it was expensive. A big standup radio could cost $250 to $300. My uncle subscribed to the Waco *News-Tribune*. It was a great thing to read once a day.

Probably the two most popular callers to any farm were the Raleigh Man and the Watkins Man, who traveled the rural areas selling spices, threads, and all kinds of things. The reason we looked forward to seeing the Raleigh Man and the Watkins Man was not for the goods they brought, but for the news from other people and places. They were like kinfolks to us, and Aunt Mittie always bought at least a little something from them, just to have their company for a while. They usually stayed a couple of hours, sometimes taking a meal with us. We kids preferred the Raleigh Man because he was a little more liberal with candy. He had a Model "T" Ford truck equipped with a cabinet-type contraption in which he carried his wares. On top of this was a wire chicken pen. Often the farmer's wife had no cash, and the peddler traded goods for chickens, eggs, fresh hog meat, or anything else of value.

Another man who came about five times a year was Mr. Goolsby, a cattle trader. When he rolled up in his big old truck, all work ceased while he and Uncle George haggled over the price of whatever hogs and cattle we had for sale. It was something to watch. There was no facility for weighing the animals, so the cattle trader had to be good at estimating by looks.

Tuesday was traditionally washday at our farm. Early in the morning the black cast iron washpot, which would hold about twenty gallons of water, was placed on bricks. A wood fire was built under it, and the water was heated to almost boiling before lye soap was added, then the dirty clothes. For half an hour or so the clothes were punched with a stick. Then they were lifted out with the stick, placed in a tub, and carried to the washbench. Water was added, and the clothes were scrubbed on a washboard. Most of the water was then squeezed out by hand, and the clothes were placed in a second tub for rinsing, squeezed again, and put into a third tub of water with some Mrs. Tucker's Bluing added (to take the dinginess out). Then the clothes were squeezed again and hung on the clothesline. This was an all-day job, and usually one of the younguns was left at the house to help with the washing. It wasn't a popular assignment, and kids always tried to look busy at picking time. In 1926 we got a hand-operated wringer to make the job easier. Still, the person who manned the washboard had red and peeling hands by the time the day was over from the harsh lye soap. But the clothes were clean.

Life on the farm wasn't without its rewards in the form of escape. Leaving the farm to go the fourteen miles into Waco was a real privilege during the week, since we didn't finish the dairying until around seven in the evening. On some Saturdays my

A school picture of Lewis from Lorena, Texas.

cousin and I would get to go to Waco at noon with a dollar each. For that dollar, I could have two hamburgers (ten cents each), two Dr Peppers (five cents each), two picture shows (fifteen cents each), two bags of popcorn (five cents each), two boxes of Cracker Jacks to take home (five cents each), and still have twenty cents left at the end of a full afternoon.

One time, in the fall of 1927, my grandmother decided that all the grandkids, about eight of us, deserved a treat. In the south part of Waco was the Cotton Palace, a yearly county fair with exhibits, a midway, contests, the works. Named for the ruling enterprise of the area, the Cotton Palace was *the* place to be in the fall.

My uncles George and Fred furnished the transportation for the big trip, two open Model "T" Fords. They would not be staying with us at the fair; instead a young female friend was to be our chaperone. She was entrusted with the money, about forty dollars, which was an enormous sum in 1927. I cannot recall if the family had had some kind of windfall or if my grandmother had simply saved loose change for a long time; I suspect it was the latter.

After a fourteen-mile ride, we arrived about eleven in the morning at the Cotton Palace, an excited group of kids looking forward to a full day. We headed for the midway first. No sooner had we reached that den of pleasure than one of the barkers at a gambling booth asked if we'd all like to win a big prize by playing an easy game. The chaperone took the bait, and within fifteen minutes we had no prize, and the gambler had all our money! This meant no rides, no food, no fun. Our day was over. We toured the exhibits but could not muster any enthusiasm for them after our crushing loss.

On our way to the main gate for our 5:00 P.M. meeting with our uncles, we saw a man giving away samples of chocolate-coated Ex-Lax. None of us knew what it was, and we all ate some. One by one, everyone got sick during the ride home. After many stops of an emergency nature, we arrived in Lorena, sadder, wiser, and weaker. A bigger bunch of country bumpkins would have been hard to find.

As winter came on each year, we all started thinking about hog-killing time; the big item in our winter diet was meat. Pork accounted for about seventy-five percent of the meat we ate, with a little chicken and beef for variety. With a big family and hired hands, it took quite a bit of food to get through the winter.

We raised our own hogs on a three- or four-acre hog patch, which had within it a covered hogpen fifty by one hundred feet. We raised corn to feed the hogs, and windmills pumped their water. If there was no wind, we pumped it by hand. The female hog, or sow, produces a litter of between seven and fifteen pigs in only eleven weeks or so. With proper care, the pigs grow rapidly to 180 to 200 pounds, and from then on, they are candidates for slaughter.

As a child I watered and fed the hogs and watched the little pigs. I even gave them nicknames, like Runt, Little 'Un, Big 'Un, Spot, and Red. I really became sort of fond of them, but I knew how important that meat was. With the first norther came hog-killing time, and I could bid my grown-up friends goodbye without much regret.

Hog-killing time was almost a festive occasion. Neighbors usually came to help in exchange for part of the product. The spot for the work was near the harness house under a large tree. There were two methods of slaughtering—shooting and stabbing—and there were always arguments about which method to use. Two large metal pots were needed to heat water, one fifty-five gallon barrel held the hot water for scalding the hog, and a block-and-tackle pulley was tied to a large limb of a nearby tree.

The hooks were put in the hamstring of the slaughtered hog, and the carcass was raised into the air and lowered into the barrel of scalding water. The barrel had to be slightly tilted so that the hog would go in and out easier. We used a long table and plenty of sharp knives, and it was important for the hog to be properly bled first. After the scalding, the hog was put on the table and the hair was scraped off with knives. Then the hog was cut up, and almost everything—brain, heart, etc.—was saved. Part of the meat was cut up and ground into sausage and stuffed into sacks, with about four to five pounds to the sack. The shoulders and hams and bacon were salted and wrapped and hung up in the smokehouse (which, incidentally, used no smoke). The intestines were made into chitterlings. Some of the fat from the hog was used for cooking lard. Some was used for making lye soap for clothes washing. There was little waste. Hog killing was an all-day project. Sometimes we slaughtered three to five hogs at once.

Now when we go to the supermarket and see the bacon, chops, hams, and all the good things, we never think about the hog. We don't wonder about his birth, his maturing, and his place in our society, as we used to when we saw them each day and watched them grow up, only to be slaughtered to fill our stomachs and get us through the winter.

Hogs are now raised in what are called pig parlors. Some never touch the ground their whole lives. They live in air conditioned comfort, and they are fed a balanced, weighted diet. They are killed by gassing in large slaughterhouses now. Somehow, the meal does not taste as good as when we slaughtered hogs on hog-killing day, a long time ago.

Even with all my farm chores, I managed to stay in school and do fairly well. As the Depression came on, clothes became a real problem. I made it through my senior year, 1930–31, with one pair of pants and a pair of shoes I kept stuffed with cardboard.

There was no money for college. Times just got tougher for everyone. Even my grandmother's boarders left when other people with a spare room got hungry and offered cheaper rent.

I remember a meeting with me, my mother, grandmother, Uncle George, and Uncle Lindy. Everyone wanted me to begin supporting the family by farming on shares with my uncle. Somehow I just knew I was not cut out to be a farmer, even though I couldn't have said at that point what it was I would be. So I continued working on Uncle George's farm through 1932, earning five dollars to seven dollars a week and board. I took a dollar for myself and gave the rest to the family. When I could, I worked at a service station on Sundays for an extra one dollar and fifty cents for clothes for myself.

In 1933 the Civilian Conservation Corps was established, and I found out that if a person was on relief, he could get into this outfit. The WPA in Lorena was hauling in gravel to fill up chuckholes in the streets, so I signed a paper declaring my family was on relief, then worked two days for WPA to qualify. It was a tough thing to do. People then were terribly embarrassed to declare themselves poor, and welfare was not to be spoken of in polite company. Now people seem to accept it as a way of life. Not then.

I was given a reporting date for the CCC. On that day I hitchhiked to Waco and signed on. They gave everyone a sack lunch, then loaded us into pre-World War I vintage passenger cars. I was sent to Camp Bullis at San Antonio and then to Fort Davis in the Davis Mountains. The pay was thirty dollars a month, five dollars for me and twenty-five dollars sent home to the folks— that was the way it worked.

The Davis Mountains are the loveliest and most desolate mountains I've ever seen. The countryside was totally undeveloped then. When we got off the train at Marfa everything had to be started from scratch. We were given a cot and a mattress sack, which we then filled with straw to keep the cold out, plus two blankets and an old pillow. Some Army men were already there when we arrived—so many came with each company to set things up a little. We had a first sergeant, captain or first lieutenant, second lieutenant, and corporal. There was some jealousy between them and us, because they were making sometimes less than we were.

At first we went through the chow line with our mess kits and took our food wherever we could find to sit or hunker down and eat. Later some money was appropriated, and we built a hall with tables for indoor eating. We dug out a space against the side of the mountain for the tents, then put in caliche flooring. The tents were about sixteen by sixteen and slept eight, but if you were lucky you could get by with only four in your tent; that was a lot more comfortable. We put a stove in the tent in the winter to help fight the cold. We had 400 young men there in two companies, from all over. I'd say about twenty-five to thirty percent of my company was Mexican-American. We worked side by side, but once we left that assignment we never saw each other again. I've seen pictures hanging on the walls of the Indian Lodge in the Davis Mountains, and I can still pick myself and some of my co-workers out. It's a strange feeling.

The ranchers and people of Fort Davis, Alpine, and Marfa looked on us as trash and were sometimes hostile to us. They called us the "tree monkeys" in a "tree Army." But the roadbuilding work was good, and we were happy to be doing something and getting paid for it. The CCC surely filled a need back then.

Once my friend Travis and I, along with some other CCC workers, got a ten-day leave from Fort Davis. We were taken by truck to Pecos, where we caught a freight train to Fort Worth. We got on in the afternoon, and it rained all night. There was only one empty boxcar on the train. One of the conductors made the people in the car let us on. When the train stopped in Big Spring, Texas, the car was unloaded of eighty men, four women, and six children. Then Travis and I caught another freight train to Waco.

After being at home about six days, Travis and I tried to catch a moving freight train out of Waco. Travis managed to get aboard, but it was moving too fast and I could not make it. Travis jumped off and in a little while, the train stopped for some reason and we got on. We intended to ride the Katy to San Antonio and catch the Southern Pacific to Alpine, but the railroad bulls kicked us off in Austin, and we spent the night in a junk car lot. We then managed to catch the Katy to Temple and rode the Santa Fe west. Finally, after three or four days of going hungry and without much sleep, we rode a freight into Pecos. Now our only problem was to get to Fort Davis, about seventy-five miles away. We started walking and walked to Balmorhea. That took us all day.

When we reached Balmorhea about seven that evening, I said, "Travis, we've got no money and I'm hungry, but I have never begged."

Travis said, "I haven't either, and I don't think I can."

I said, "By God, I'm hungrier than you," and I walked over to a combination grocery, icehouse, and meat market. I asked for the owner, and a man about fifty years old came out.

"Sir," I said, "me and Travis over there sitting in the park are hungry. We will work."

The man said, "I don't have any work tonight, but at five tomorrow morning I can use you to help load a truck of beef I'm taking to Alpine."

"Fine!" I said, and he gave me a loaf of bread (which sold for about twelve cents at the time), two pounds of bologna (sixteen cents a pound), and a half gallon of milk (about twenty-eight cents). That was the best meal I ever had.

Next morning Travis and I helped load the beef and got two donuts and coffee each and a ride to Fort Davis. The trip was a very educational experience.

After four months in the Davis Mountains we were moved to Roswell, New Mexico, to Bottomless Lakes State Park, where we built roads and a lodge. We lived there in semi-permanent barracks, with a mess hall. The people there in New Mexico were very kind to us. By that time the CCC was a little better accepted by the public, and the people of Roswell recognized the fact that we brought money into the community as well as building something they needed.

I was discharged from the CCC in 1934 and moved to Oklahoma City to live with my Uncle Lindy and his family. Times were still very hard. Uncle Lindy got me a job selling appliances on commission at Oklahoma Tire and Supply Company. I spent three and a half days on the floor, and the rest of the time canvassing homes for prospects. By late 1934, I could see that I could not make it selling appliances. I hitchhiked back to Lorena and worked for eight months on the farm and at a service station.

In 1935 I enlisted in the U. S. Army, 15th Field Artillery, and was sent to San Antonio. I was paid twenty-one dollars a month and sent a fourteen dollar allotment to my folks back home. The irony was that I was back at Camp Bullis, not forty yards from where I'd slept in that CCC tent. And I was making nine dollars a month less than I had as a "tree monkey." But those three years in the Army turned out to be my real education. I learned how to survive. I learned how to get along with people, and I became a good judge of character.

In the Army of those days, there were only two trades a young man could learn—being a truck driver or a cook. I knew that wasn't where I wanted to be, so I began to scuffle to make extra money and get ready to run my own life. When I won seventy dollars in a dice game, I became a money lender in the Army. The going rate then was twenty to twenty-five percent a month. With forty dollars of my profit, I bought a concession for pickup and delivery of laundry, which paid eight dollars a week. Then I bought an old car and started renting it out. I began buying canteen checks issued in five dollar, seven dollars and fifty cents, and ten dollar books, paying seventy-five percent in real money for them. The latter part of the month I was able to sell the books for a twenty percent profit.

I was promoted to PFC and then to Corporal. With a salary of a whopping forty-two dollars a month, I raised my allotment home to thirty dollars. I thought I would be staying in the Army for good, but on a three-day pass to Dallas, I met Leah Viola Mahachek, a nurse, and all my plans changed. We married in

November, 1935: Private Lewis Rigler, 15th Field Artillery, Battery A, Fort Sam Houston, Texas.

Lewis Rigler (second from right) with the 15th Field Artillery at Fort Sam Houston

In early 1942, Lewis Rigler as a member of the Texas Highway Patrol, Dallas, Texas.

Lewis Rigler (right) with his partner James P. Atkinson, Jr., Texas Highway Patrol 1943, Grand Prairie, Texas.

Below, a 4'x115' tower escorted by Rigler & W. F. Todd on motorcycles from Dallas to Wichita Falls, Texas, "raining all the way," according to the inscription.

1937, with twenty-two dollars between us, ten dollars of which we spent on a wedding ring. I was discharged from the Army in 1938.

Leah was a surgical nurse at Dallas' Baylor Hospital. She mostly supported us in the early days. I sold vacuum cleaners door to door and worked at a service station. Then I entered Texas A&M College in 1939, to study veterinary science. Leah took a job at the college hospital. When our first son was born in 1940, finances became a problem again. After another year, I quit school, took a competitive exam with the Department of Public Safety, and became a drivers license examiner. The pay was $125 a month. We had another son in 1942. That year I was transferred into the Highway Patrol, and we moved to Grand Prairie, where our third son was born in 1943. Leah became a public school nurse, and we bought our first home. In 1947, I received a Texas Ranger appointment and was assigned to Company B, stationed at Gainesville. There we moved, and there I have remained.

The boys grew up and were just setting out on their own when Leah had a stroke in 1960 and died quite suddenly. I felt that I would never marry again, but some time later I met a young divorcee, Joyce Tucker Tempel, with five small daughters. I started all over again as a father when Joyce and I were married in 1963, and I think it has kept me young.

On August 31, 1977, I retired from the Department of Public Safety after thirty-six years of service, thirty of them with the Rangers. For about four years, I worked in public relations and security with a Gainesville financial institution. I am now employed part time as a consultant in my son's CPA firm and along with my wife run an investment company. I also co-own a bail bond business. I am not a man who can adjust to having no regular work outside the home; I just seem to enjoy keeping busy.

When I look back on it all, I believe that my family and I have endured, even prospered, partly because I decided early in life to accept what I'd been given, to make the best of it that I could to get by, but most of all to prevail. I always knew I'd make it, even in my work. That knowledge made each day challenging and interesting. Now I can look back with pleasure and pride on a career of service and a life of great happiness.

Lewis Rigler signing his book at his office. Above his desk is a photograph of his three boys, from left to right: Erik, Mike, Steven

4

The Clover Seed Siege

One early evening in March of 1956, I came home to find my three teenage boys watching a TV program about two policemen trying to get a mentally ill man out of a house where he'd barricaded himself. If you remember the police shows of the 1950s and 1960s (*Dragnet, The Naked City*), you know they were pretty awful. The unreal quality of most of them, with gun slinging and high drama, has probably done more harm than good to the lawman's image. It's funny—very few men in law enforcement enjoy shoot-'em-up type police shows. Maybe we think it's overdone, maybe we just don't care to see any more of it after working it all day, I don't know. I *do* know we rarely have the kind of dramatic confrontation the TV shows portray as commonplace.

I teased the boys some about watching such trash. They kidded me back about how I would handle a situation like that. Just about the time the show ended, the phone rang. It was Sheriff Wiley Barnes of Denton, about thirty miles south of Gainesville. "Lewis," he asked, "can you come help me in the morning? I've got a crazy man down here holed up on his farm, threatening to kill a bunch of people."

The man (I'll call him Jenkins) had taken over the operation of the family farm after his father's death five or six years before. He had recently bought an adjoining farm and was working both places. He'd gotten his degree not long before, he had a wife and an eighteen-month-old baby girl, and he was known as a hard worker and a man of unquestionable character. Local people described him as a loner, though, and he was thought to have been having some mental problems for several weeks.

About two days before Sheriff Barnes called me, Jenkins began this bizarre battle by threatening his wife and child, and eventually, running them off the farm. He had threatened a service station operator in Sanger as well, and when several people came by to try to reason with him he brandished a gun and said he'd use it, and he had a reputation as a crack shot. Since he'd begun this strange behavior, he'd been doing quite a bit of target practice there on the farm.

After she and the baby left, Jenkins' wife had called his mother in California, and the mother had taken a plane to Fort Worth. Jenkins himself had met his mother's plane. While on their way back to the farm they were stopped by three police cars sent out to apprehend Jenkins, but he had a gun and refused to surrender. He even stepped out of the car to threaten the men with the gun, saying he'd just as soon kill them all as go to jail.

The presence of Jenkins' mother in the car made his apprehension more difficult. She somehow managed to talk to one of the officers while her son was yelling at the others. She convinced the officer that if they'd let her and her son return to Sanger, she'd get the gun away from him that night and they could make an arrest the next morning. The officer didn't seem to have any other choice, so he reluctantly agreed.

Sheriff Barnes asked my advice. I told him I'd meet him in Sanger the next morning an hour before sunup. I always preferred making arrests of this type about daybreak. I've handled dangerous, mentally ill people many times and no two are alike.

The one constant is the volatility of the situation. A little bit of psychology will usually do more good than a lot of force.

I have had many calls like this, and few of them have worried me, but somehow this one was different. I thought about it a while, then called Captain Bob Crowder in Dallas and asked that an armored car be sent to Sanger, in case we needed it. He told me to go on down to Sanger the next morning and check out the situation. If trouble developed, I could call for the car then, he said. I didn't much like that idea, but I accepted it.

I slept very little, instead using those quiet hours to work out a plan. I decided that my best bet would be to dress and look as much like a farmer as I could. I was raised on a farm, even had my own for a while. I understand farmers.

When I left Gainesville at 4:30 A.M., it was cool and clear. I was wearing old pants, a work shirt, a faded jacket, boots, and an old snap-brim hat. I had on two forty-five automatics, with a smaller gun concealed in my jacket pocket.

By the time I got to Sanger (about twenty miles south of Gainesville) there were seven or eight police cars, marked and unmarked, with about twenty men in them. A small army. It was all business—no one joked about this one. The sheriff and I seemed to be the unofficial leaders. We all set off toward the farm, and when we got to within a mile of it, we sent an unmarked car by the house to look things over. By then it was just getting light. I looked around a bit. The farm appeared to be above average in the care it had been given. The land was well-tended and neat. We were parked adjacent to an open field of about fifty acres. It had not been tilled and looked to be pasture land.

When the car returned from its scouting mission, the officer said they'd seen a man walking toward a barn some 500 yards from the house. I told Sheriff Barnes that if he and one of his deputies would accompany me, I would drive up to the subject and we would try to take him without gunplay.

I couldn't get out of my mind two coincidental facts: The sheriff had just recovered from being shot in the stomach by a deranged person (he had been in serious condition for some time and still was not back to 100 percent), and the sheriff preceding him had been blinded by a shot from an insane man.

We started toward the house. We hadn't gone very far when we met Jenkins' mother driving at a good clip toward us in his car. She didn't seem to want to stop at all, but we flagged her down. She was terribly frightened.

"He's still got the gun," she hollered out the window. "He says he won't be taken. I was afraid he'd kill me."

"Why didn't you get the gun away from him last night?" I asked.

"How could I? He stayed up all night, just rambling about all kinds of things, not making any sense. When he set out for the field a few minutes ago, I decided to get out."

I knew that her presence would probably make a bad situation worse. "You did the right thing, Mrs. Jenkins," I said. "Maybe you'd better go into Sanger and wait. I promise you we won't hurt your son."

She drove off. A couple of police cars followed her. The rest stayed behind Wiley and me at a distance. After seeing her, I knew all the plans I had made the night before were useless. This was a new predicament; what I had hoped would be the arrest of an unarmed man was something else now.

We headed toward the house again. When we got near, we saw Jenkins walking across a field about 250 yards away. Fences and plowed ground prevented driving any farther into the field. We stopped and got out, and everyone took cover behind the cars. Then Jenkins spotted us. He came right toward us, taking long strides. He was a tall man, about six feet one inch, 180 pounds. Thirty yards from us, he stopped.

"You're under arrest, Jenkins!" someone called out.

I didn't think that was too smart, but then nobody asked me. I suppose it might have worked—you have to try.

Jenkins hollered back, "I'm just out here hunting rabbits on my own land. You're the ones don't belong here. If anybody tries to arrest me, I'll shoot about six of you. Now get out of here!"

I believed he meant it.

There was a minute of deathly silence. Then I heard the sound of crying. I looked and saw Jenkins' mother running across the field to her son, crying that he should surrender. She must have had second thoughts after leaving. She came up to him, still crying out, and threw herself at him, even trying to catch the hand that held the gun. He pushed her away roughly. I could hear him shout at her: "Leave me alone, or I'll kill you, too! You're just like the rest—you're all against me!"

About this time I heard a rifle click as a shell was pushed into its chamber. The officer next to me had his rifle pointed at Jenkins; as good a marksman as he was, and at that distance, I felt sure he would kill or badly hurt the man if he fired.

"Officer," I said softly, "please hold your fire. I want to try something."

Suddenly I knew that I could handle this situation—why, I don't know, even now. Somehow I sensed that this man wouldn't hurt me.

"Mr. Jenkins," I yelled, "would you shoot a man if he had his hands up?"

"Well, I *might*!" he hollered back. I could hear the anger in him.

I took a deep breath and stepped out from behind the car with my hands raised. He looked at me and I looked at him. The sheriff and the other fifteen or so officers there might just as well have left.

"Mr. Jenkins," I called, "I want to talk to you, but not with these guns on. I'm gonna take them off and leave 'em here."

He said nothing. I unbuckled my gun belt and laid my guns on the trunk of the car.

"Do you believe I'm unarmed now?" I yelled.

"I guess I do," he answered warily.

"I've got one more gun in my jacket pocket, Mr. Jenkins. I just wouldn't feel right talking to you with it on, so I'm gonna put it here on the car, too."

Again he said nothing. I took out the gun and laid it on the car.

"Now I'm gonna take off my jacket and let you see I've got no more guns on me. I trust you so completely that I'll even turn my back on you. I don't think you want to harm me."

I turned all the way around. Slowly, so he could get a good look at me.

"Maybe you're okay," he hollered, "but the others sure aren't. I'm not doin' any talkin' while they're out there drawin' a bead on me."

"I think you're real smart, Mr. Jenkins," I yelled back. I asked the other men to lay down their guns. They all looked at Sheriff Barnes. He waited a minute. Then he reached over and laid his shotgun on the car hood. The others took their guns off and put them on their trunks or hoods.

Across the distance between us, I could see Jenkins ease up a bit. I began to talk to him then, hollering across those ninety feet. We talked about the problems of farming—about putting everything you have into the land, working all day and usually half the night, and never knowing if you'd make a penny when it was all over. All the time, I was edging forward. We talked about watching your calves die and not being able to do anything to save them. We talked about raising the best crop you can and getting so little for it that you wondered why you bothered. I could feel the other peace officers watching me. I wasn't sure all of them approved of my way of doing it, and I could understand that, especially after what had happened to two sheriffs in this county at the hands of disturbed people. But I knew our only chance was for me to keep talking. And as we talked, I felt I could understand his bitterness over the hard life of a farmer. Then suddenly I was no longer worried about what might happen to me. Just about what might happen to him.

"I can't even get sixteen dollars a hundredweight for 1,600 pounds of the best clover seed you ever saw," Jenkins yelled.

So there it was.

"I've been looking to buy some clover seed myself," I hollered back, "and that sounds like a fair price to me. If we can take a look at that seed and it's as good as you say it is, I'll buy it right now. Would you take a check?"

"I guess I would," he yelled, and I started toward him. Then there was just the fence between us, three strands of barbed wire. Both of us started down toward his barn to look at the seed. His mother followed. She was smart enough to keep quiet this time.

We walked along, him on one side of the barbed wire, me on the other, not talking for a few minutes. I could still feel the eyes of my fellow officers on our backs. I remember hoping they wouldn't do anything foolish just because they were afraid for me. I thought about climbing that barbed wire fence, but I couldn't see that it would help me any. It might spook Jenkins, though by now I doubted it as he seemed so calm. But then it might spook the men watching us. I can remember touching the cedar posts as we passed them.

I knew I had to get that gun away from him. "Mr. Jenkins," I said over the fence, "it just doesn't seem fair that you and I might be fixing to make a deal on this seed and you still have a gun and I don't."

"I guess you're right," he said. "When we get to the house, I'll get rid of it."

I was surprised how soft-spoken he was now that we were close to each other and didn't have to holler.

"I believe you mean that," I said.

He looked at me. "I'm a man of my word."

We turned and went on up along the fence toward his house and barn. We had gone about 500 yards with the fence between us; then it ended, and we were at the gate. He stopped there, then came and met me in the open. Suddenly he ejected the clip from his gun, took the bullet out of the barrel, and put the gun in his pocket.

We went on down to the barn to look at the clover seed. I could see his mother heading for the house. We went into the barn, and I looked the seed over carefully.

"Just the kind of seed I've been looking for, Mr. Jenkins," I said, "the right amount, too. Do you happen to have a blank-check on you?"

"I reckon so," he said, rummaging around in his shirt pocket until he found one.

I filled out the check for $256, as agreed upon, using a barrel in the barn for a writing surface. I handed him the check, and we shook hands.

He seemed to have completely calmed down. I felt that he looked upon me now as maybe the closest thing to a friend he'd had in a long time. We started back toward the house. I knew it had to be now.

"Mr. Jenkins," I said, "I hate to bring this up, but you know you've had charges filed against you, and we need to go into town to make bond. Why don't we take your car? You can drive, and your mother can come along. We'll stop at the bank in Sanger and cash this check."

"I guess that'll be okay," he said.

We got in the car, and he gave me the gun. Jenkins seemed

calm and his mother relieved. Me, I was elated. He drove those four miles pretty fast. Several cars followed us in, but he didn't seem to mind. The bank in Sanger was still closed when we got to town, so we drove on to Denton. We shook hands again in the sheriff's office, and I left him there and went home.

When I wrote my memorandum on the case to Captain Crowder, I added a postscript to the letter accompanying it: "P.S. If you are interested, I know where 1,600 pounds of clover seed can be procured at a *very reasonable* figure. L.C.R." The check I had given Jenkins was taken from him at the county jail and mailed to me later by Chief Deputy Bud Gentle. Attached to it was a note typed on Denton County Sheriff's Office stationery. It said, "Ranger Rigler, Gainesville, Texas. Pardner, here is your check. Thanks a lot. Bud Gentle." I still have the check.

Jenkins was treated in a mental institution for several months and then released. Sometime within the year following the incident, I got a call from Sheriff Barnes.

"Jenkins is back at home and causing trouble again," he said. "You might want to see if you can do anything. You seem to be the only one he might listen to."

I drove first to Sanger and found out that Jenkins' family had left again and that he'd been seen on his property with firearms, just as before. Then I went on to Denton. I suggested that we send him a jury summons, which we did on a Thursday. When he came to court on Monday, I was there. He recognized me immediately and seemed perfectly comfortable.

"We meet again, Mr. Jenkins," I said.

"Looks that way," he said.

"It seems like the problem is about the same, and I believe you might need a little help again, sir," I said. "We've got to go on down and get this cleared up."

"That's fine, Ranger. Let's go," he said calmly.

We had a nice visit that day. Not a word passed between us about the previous incident or the seed. Jenkins was committed again to the Terrell mental facility. He stayed for a brief period and then was released again.

Five years later, Jenkins was killed on the City of Denton courthouse lawn by local police. It was said that he had a gun and was after the sheriff to return the guns taken from him in the earlier arrest. It was reported that he fired three shots at officers; doctors found six bullet wounds in his chest.

I felt a deep sadness. The man was young, a good worker, and just had mental problems. I felt almost a kinship with this troubled man. In a few brief moments I had saved his life and he had saved mine. I only regret that I never took the time to build a friendship with him.

I shall remember forever that no one was hurt in the incident that early March morning. I guess I received more praise and notoriety for that one act, including mention in the *Congressional Record,* than for any other in my entire career. I did not then, nor do I now, consider it to have been a particularly brave act on my part. It just seemed the proper thing to do.

This sort of situation comes up somewhere in our land over and over again. Officers before me have handled crises such as this in a similar fashion. Now officers are specially trained as crisis negotiators. Any officer who is a good one wants much, much more to save a life than to take one. If I had not been a good public speaker and a halfway con artist, I would not have been successful that morning. I originally questioned the need for including this incident in my story, but finally decided it provides an insight into the varied duties and responsibilities of an officer.

Lewis Rigler's first murder case in Gainesville in 1948. A man was killed above the bakery on E. California Street.

5

Two Little Girls

Of all the violent crimes I've seen during my years of law enforcement, those involving children are by far the most difficult to work. Even now, after having seen it again and again, and having developed the "thick skin" necessary for dealing with brutality without simply going mad, I consider the kind of sickness required to hurt a child deliberately almost beyond the imagination. Seeing the results of this particular kind of sick mind gone wild can sadden and depress a man more than just about anything else, to a point nearly past reason.

Such was my mental state after September 11, 1969, when I was called to Sherman, in Grayson County, to join the search for a missing girl. I worked fourteen hours that day, but it was only the beginning of an investigation that was to last more than seven months and affect the lives of many people. Though I knew none of those involved personally, my life would be changed forever by what I was to see over those months.

Donna Marie Golish, age seven, disappeared on her way home from Fairview Elementary School in northwest Sherman on September 10, 1969. Ordinarily, Donna walked home through a small park and a grove of trees, about a twenty-minute walk.

She usually walked with a girlfriend, but the girl had broken her arm the day before and did not go to school that day. When Donna failed to come home for lunch as usual, her stepmother first called the school to confirm that Donna had left there for home at the usual time, then searched the neighborhood for the little girl. By early afternoon, Mrs. Golish had called Donna's father home, reported the little girl missing, and local officers had begun a search for her. I was called in and joined the search about 8:00 o'clock the following morning.

About 11:30, we found Donna's body in high grass in an oilfield area about a mile and a half north of the school, two and a half miles by road. Her body was badly mutilated; it appeared that she had been hit on the head and then run over by an automobile. She was wearing only a slip, pushed high on her body; none of her other clothing, except her shoes, was found at the scene. Fragments of paint were imbedded in the heel of one of Donna's feet, and a small amount of oil was found on the same foot.

After conducting a crime scene search with Grayson County Sheriff G. W. (Woody) Blanton, Chief of Police J. Burleson, and other officers, taking photographs and measurements and double checking for evidence, I participated in an intensive investigation. School officials and teachers, children who could have seen Donna, neighbors, and family members were questioned—anyone who might have seen anything, however insignificant it may have seemed at the time, which could help us track down Donna's murderer. The crime scene was searched again and again. The bloodstained grass and soil, as well as Donna's shoes and the paint fragments from her foot, were sent to the FBI Laboratory in Washington, D. C., for analysis.

From the beginning we had the feeling there was not much to go on, and we were right. The days stretched into weeks without a solid lead. We worked ten to fourteen hours per day interviewing, rechecking facts, and searching desperately for a good clue.

Our best lead came from two six-year-old boys who lived near Donna. Fairview Park was on the way home for all of them, and the boys had entered the park about five minutes ahead of Donna. Both saw a car parked there, and though it was difficult to get a very clear description from six-year-olds, we were able to tell that the car had perhaps been a Comet, Tempest, Falcon, or F-85, and that its color was beige. Both agreed that the radio aerial was broken, and that the car had several stickers on the bumper and one in the rear window. They argued for a time about what they had seen, but finally we ascertained that as they had approached the car, they had split, one walking on each side. The boys said that the car's motor was running, and a young man with long sideburns was sitting with his feet out of the car.

Several times in newspaper articles and on the radio, we appealed to the public for help in finding the killer, believing that it could be someone from around the area and that the continued publicity would put pressure on that could eventually result in a break. The reports of our investigation began to stack up—within a month of the murder I had one hundred pages of information in my file alone. We had questioned at least a score of suspects and interviewed hundreds more. As Sheriff Blanton said in an interview published on October 19, 1969, "I have checked cars, checked rumors, checked out information people have given us. I have talked to people who live around the school who may have seen or heard something. I have compared this bit of information with that bit. But so far, everything we have done has hit a blind alley."

Even though the autopsy report showed that no sexual attack had occurred, everyone felt that the murderer was a man. A Sherman radio station offered $500, and three persons anonymously offered a $700 reward for information leading to the arrest and conviction of the person responsible for the brutal murder of the little girl.

One of the prime suspects was an individual known in the area as the "Doll Man," a retired railroad employee in his sixties. Mentally unbalanced, the Doll Man made a habit of purchasing large dolls and then mutilating them in a perverted way. Several of his discarded dolls had been found in San Angelo, where he lived before moving to Denison, and others had turned up in Sherman. He had also been accused of molesting young girls and of indecent exposure. We talked with doctors who had treated the Doll Man on various occasions and interviewed salespeople in stores where he may have bought dolls. Though we didn't have enough information to subject him to questioning or a polygraph, I still felt that he could be our man, and we continued to follow up on any lead concerning the Doll Man.

After more than six months of almost fruitless work, it began to look as though we would never find Donna's murderer. The investigation was still active the following spring when a similar murder occurred nearby.

On April 1, 1970, eleven-year-old Francis Laurese (Laurie) Stevens, who lived east of Denison, which is eight or nine miles north of Sherman, was reported missing when she, too, failed to appear at home after leaving Lamar School. Laurie had last been seen at 3:30 P.M., walking east in the 700 block of E. Shepherd, only three blocks from home. Her brother later found her purse and books about fifty feet from where a schoolmate had said goodbye and left Laurie to continue home. About three feet away from the books, in the pasture beside the road, freshly made footprints were found, large enough to be a man's.

We searched for four days before Laurie's body was found in a ravine near Randell Lake, northwest of Denison, by two servicemen stationed at nearby Perrin Air Force Base.

The child's body, which was face down when discovered,

had been punctured by six bullet wounds from a small caliber pistol. She had been stripped of her clothing, except for her black patent shoes and white socks, but it did not appear that she had been sexually molested (the autopsy later confirmed this). Her hands were carefully placed beneath her head, as if to protect her face from the leaves and dirt in the ravine, and her legs were crossed at the ankles.

Photographs and measurements were taken, and the crime scene search began. Most of the girl's clothing was found in a nearby ditch. On the east side of the road, scuff marks were found on the roadside leading into a pasture, along with one partial footprint, believed to be that of a man. We also discovered one small footprint, believed to be the girl's. On the west bank of the ravine we found the heel print of a man's shoe. No spent cartridges were found, but we did locate tire tracks nearby. We worked about five hours at the crime scene before briefing the news media. It was a long, hard search. We decided to dig up about eight inches of the moist dirt from the ditch in which the body lay to turn over to the sheriff's department investigator. I dug up almost all the earth we took for evidence. I remember saying during the deposition later that I did ninety percent of the digging with a shovel obtained from the nearby water treatment station and that I could recall the digging very well because I finally "gave out" doing it.

After we left the scene, Sheriff Blanton and I had to go and give the news to the girl's mother and stepfather. I knew that since Laurie had been missing for several days, her parents were probably somewhat prepared for the truth, but that didn't make our task any easier. We were with the parents for thirty or forty minutes, and it was very difficult to tell them what we had found. They had no idea who might have wanted to hurt their daughter.

The next day was a Sunday, and Sheriff Blanton and I were so emotionally spent after working twelve- to fifteen-hour days that week that we decided to take Sunday off so we could start fresh on Monday checking out leads. I went home very late Saturday night and tried to rest. All day Sunday I tried to relax and enjoy being with my family, but it was impossible to forget the sight of that child lying in the ditch.

Monday morning I was back in Denison. In five two-man teams, we began checking out leads. Sheriff's investigator Jerry Cleveland and I decided to reopen our investigation of the Doll Man. We spent all day matching discarded dolls with sales slips and interviewing department store personnel about the man who had bought them. We interviewed the Doll Man the following day at the Department of Public Safety office in Dallas. At that time we also did a polygraph test, which he passed. We had spent a great deal of time on the Doll Man, and it looked as if it had all been a waste. I was very disappointed.

Other leads were not resulting in the same dead end, however. A car which had been repeatedly seen near the murder site, both before and after the crime, started turning up in the interviews of more and more people—a 1968 red Chevrolet with a bent right front fender. The car had been seen around the Lamar schoolyard in Denison, and on nearby Shepherd Street where Laurie lived, on several occasions, parked or cruising slowly, wasting time—looking for trouble, so to speak. The driver of the Chevrolet had also been seen riding a motorcycle in the area, on the route Laurie took from school to home; someone had even seen him pushing the motorcycle through the alley behind the Stevens' home several times.

All descriptions of the young man matched. Many people knew who he was, 18-year-old Charles Denis Oliver Easley; those who didn't concurred in their descriptions of him as round-faced, with long, shaggy hair and sideburns. The pieces began to fit together.

On April 4, some few hours before Laurie's body was discovered, the red Chevrolet had been seen driving at high speed away from what turned out to be the spot where the body was found. Since it is quite common for a killer to loiter near the area where he has killed his victim or placed the body, we knew that this young man's presence was important. Sometimes this "killer returning to the scene of the crime" syndrome takes on rather bizarre characteristics. Murderers have been known to go to the graveyard where a victim is buried and literally roll in the fresh dirt heaped upon the grave. Sometimes they come back for pieces of clothing, "souvenirs" of their crime.

After we began looking for others who had seen the young man in the red Chevrolet, a man contacted us with another helpful bit of information. He had been driving on Randell Lake Drive late in the afternoon of April 1, the day Laurie was killed, and had been run off the roadway by a young man in a red Chevrolet matching Easley's description. The spot where the car was run off the road was located, confirmed, measured, and found to be approximately eight-tenths of a mile from the spot where Laurie's body was found. The next time the car was spotted in the area, the license number was recorded. Circumstantial evidence continued to mount up.

One of Easley's neighbors had seen him and his brother repainting the door of the red Chevrolet late in the evening of April 1, the day of the murder. The paint was red, but the door came out lighter than the original paint job.

By this time, residents of the area could think of little besides the fact that a child murderer was loose out there somewhere. Real panic set in. Little girls were no longer allowed to walk home from school, but were picked up by their anxious parents instead.

Our break finally came when the red Chevrolet was spotted at a service station and Easley left without paying for his gasoline. The next morning, April 8, 1970, Easley was arrested for petty theft of gasoline. His car was impounded and searched. The car was dusted for fingerprints, vacuumed out, and thoroughly searched. Dirt and leaves were sacked up and sent to the lab. In the glove compartment I found a checkbook and a map of Sherman, but nothing really helpful.

During the next few days, almost forty witnesses to Easley's activities were interviewed—from friends of the suspect to schoolmates of the victim, neighbors, etc. When we discovered that Charles Easley had had at his disposal the previous September a Pontiac Tempest, and that a car answering that description had been seen parked and loitering near the school from which Donna Marie Golish had disappeared, in the same manner as the red Chevrolet, we thought for the first time we might really have our man. The two six-year-old boys who had seen the strange young man in the beige car were able to pick Easley out of a lineup.

Finally, the word of a woman in Sherman who had been Easley's neighbor for the approximately six months he'd lived in that city added fuel to the growing fire. Though Easley had washed the beige 1963 Tempest quite frequently as a rule, on the day of the Golish murder this neighbor had seen him washing the Tempest at least six or seven times. For several weeks after that day, he had washed it between two and five times daily. Another link in our chain of circumstantial evidence was that Easley had moved from Denison to Sherman about a month before the Golish girl was killed and that he had returned to Denison less than two months before the Stevens slaying.

The Tempest was then impounded and searched. Everything the boys had described, down to the broken aerial, matched. Paint from underneath the car was sent to the ATF (Treasury Department's Alcohol, Tobacco and Firearms Division) laboratory in Washington, D. C., along with the paint fragments found on Donna Golish's foot. The paint matched, and upon further research, it was found that the batch of paint with that chemical content was used on about 200 Tempests. The lab technician would later be used to testify as to how many Tempests were made and how many were still in operation, etc. It was still all circumstantial but it was as strong as that kind of evidence could get.

Finally, formal charges were filed against Easley in the Stevens murder. Shortly afterwards, a woman called and said that she had given the police Easley's name several months before on the Golish investigation because he had tried to pick up her little girl and she had run from him. He was driving the 1963 Pontiac Tempest.

Easley had a .22 caliber pistol with him when he was arrested. Laurie Stevens was shot with a .22 caliber weapon. However, Easley's gun could not be positively identified as the one that fired the bullets dug out of the Stevens girl's body; it was made of such poor metal that every bullet fired came out a different way. Easley later told someone in jail that he had run a drill through the barrel to make a ballistics comparison impossible. Other inmates said that Easley bragged about having killed two people. He also wrote a confession in jail and sent it to the sheriff, but it was ruled inadmissible in court.

On April 16, 1970, round-faced, shaggy-haired, eighteen-year-old Charles Denis Oliver Easley, the son of a laborer and a school dropout, was indicted on two counts of murder. At the time he was charged with the murders, three willful burning cases were pending against him in county court. We guessed that he may have been trying to set the fires to burn up evidence in the pasture.

During my deposition I had a chance to make a statement that has stuck with me ever since, and it apparently made quite an impression at the time. Actually, it represented my feeling in all my law enforcement work. As the last question in my testimony, Robert Richardson, representing the state of Texas, asked: "Has anybody told you how to testify in this case, Ranger Rigler?" I replied: "Mr. Richardson, nobody would dare."

Easley's case was tried with purely circumstantial evidence; we could never really establish a motive for the murders. He was convicted, and on July 14, 1970, in Wichita Falls, Easley received a 300-year sentence for the Stevens murder. After the Stevens trial, but before the Golish trial, Easley's lawyer said to those on the prosecution side, "If you can prove to me that he did it, I'll plead him guilty." Sheriff Blanton took the lawyer out in his car, drove the entire route, and showed the lawyer how he thought Easley killed the Golish girl. The lawyer either wasn't convinced or just couldn't bring himself to plead his client guilty.

The jury had no such qualms; Easley was found guilty and received the death sentence in McKinney for the Golish murder on March 31, 1971. Unfortunately, some strange circumstances surrounding this trial resulted in the judge failing to render a final verdict, and the resolution of the case remained unofficial. In the meantime, the Wichita Falls verdict had been reversed. Easley was tried again on the Stevens murder and received 100 years. Easley was retried for the Golish murder in April, 1975, at Victoria. On November 12, 1975, the Texas Court of Criminal Appeals held that the evidence was insufficient for conviction in the Stevens case, and the charges were dropped. On the Golish murder retrial, a Dallas judge on November 24, 1975, found Easley guilty and gave him a life sentence. When the case was appealed again in 1978, the Supreme Court refused to review it and upheld the life sentence.

When this case was finally closed, I felt great relief that it was over at last. It had been painful and frustrating from beginning to end, and I was grateful that I could move on to something else, something less brutal in nature, I hoped. I knew, though, for the parents of those two little girls, the agony of the ordeal would never end.

Perhaps the greatest irony of the two deaths came when deputy sheriffs were going through Laurie Stevens' desk at Lamar

Elementary. There they found a drawing of a car driven by a man, with a little girl standing outside. The drawing was headed by this warning scrawled in her child's hand: "Live a little— don't get into cars with strangers."

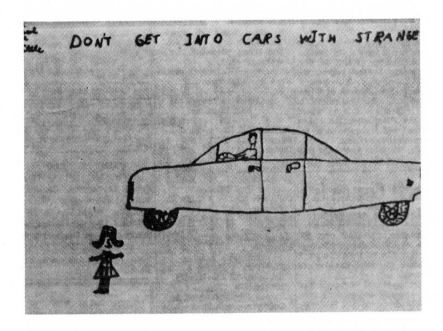

The drawing found in Laurie Stevens's desk.
"Live a little—don't get into cars with strangers."

The Rough Edges

In 1932, I was involved in my first strike. I was eighteen that year and working for a threshing outfit called McBrayer and Evans. In those days crews traveled around the country, hiring themselves out to farmers who needed help in threshing oats. The man who owned the thresher usually needed seven or eight bundle wagons to bring the oats up to the thresher. He would pay the wagon and team two dollars a day and the driver two dollars a day.

Under the heading of "fringe benefits," those of us on the work crew were furnished a cook shack where we ate, and we slept in the wagon. The work was hard, and we became convinced after a few days of it that we deserved more pay. One day a bunch of us got carried away with how important we were and how much we were needed and decided to strike for two dollars and fifty cents a day.

After the noon meal, the spokesman for us strikers told the operator, Sandy McBrayer, that we were striking for fifty cents more a day. Well, Sandy was a big, old Scotsman, about six feet four inches tall. He got out in the dirt and drew a big line with the toe of his boot. Then he said, "Now, everybody that wants to work, step across this line."

All but a few of us stepped across. I still believed that we'd get that extra money by holding out, so I stayed where I was. Mr. McBrayer (we called him Old Man McBrayer behind his back) shot the strikers a mean look and yelled, "The rest of you s.o.b.'s are fired!"

When I got home, my uncle George told me that the mules were smarter than we strikers were! That was my first strike, and I lost it. Things were a lot simpler then.

As a Ranger, I was called upon several times to uphold order in strike situations, which could become quite complicated. I never liked the work, for we were like unwanted referees in a fight. The two sides in a strike situation are like longtime marriage partners. They need each other to be happy, and no matter how serious their disagreement may seem, you know they will get back together again after all the hubbub ends. The smartest thing a law officer can do is to try to stay out of their way. But that's not always easy.

The two longest-running strikes I worked were both at Lone Star Steel. The Lone Star plant is four or five miles outside Daingerfield at a little spot called Lone Star. The picture of the Lone Star Steel plant in the *Texas Almanac* shows the fence around the plant, with pretty red flowers growing on it. The caption says, "Roses and clover curtain the rougher edges of steelmaking in the Lone Star Steel plant near Daingerfield, Texas." In my memory, nothing can curtain the rough edges of what went on around that plant when I was working those strikes.

Founded about the time of World War II as part of the war mobilization by Dallas financier and industrialist E. B. Germany, known to many as a staunch anti-laborite, Lone Star Steel continues to use most of the iron ore produced in Texas. Limonite and other East Texas iron ores are mined from open pits in Cass, Cherokee, Morris, and Nacogdoches Counties for use in the iron and steel industry at Lone Star Steel in Morris County. Before Lone Star Steel, the only industry in that area of East Texas was the making of whiskey and the raising of sweet potatoes. The steel plant literally revolutionized the area, and all the people in that part of the state became dependent upon the industry for their living.

The strike which began in the fall of 1957 and lasted forty-three days at Lone Star Steel was a wildcat strike, without union sanction. Only about half the workers, 1,500 men, walked out of the Lone Star plant in protest of the company's handling of grievances. Because rumors flowed back and forth between workers and nonworkers, the situation became particularly bad, sometimes leading to a falling out among kinfolk.

Sometimes now, remembering that strike, I think that the union itself implanted the idea of a strike, even though on paper they didn't sanction it. They had friends in the steel plants of Alabama and Pennsylvania, which were closed down. As soon as the strike was underway, cars came rolling into East Texas loaded with guys ready to work, with plenty of clothes in their cars. The plant moved in tents and cots and erected a big cafeteria for the "scabs" being housed there. The company hired strikebreakers and "permanently fired" all of the strikers.

About forty Highway Patrolmen and twenty Rangers worked this strike. Even though it was a wildcat strike, the union lawyers and officials were there in force. They occupied half the rooms of the Hilltop Motel in Daingerfield, and law enforcement people had the other half.

The Ranger became the bastard in this strike situation. The union didn't like him; the company didn't like him. Lone Star Steel felt that the Ranger never did as much as they wanted him to in maintaining order. I remember taking my wife Joyce with me once after that strike was settled so she could see where I'd spent all that time. It seemed ironic that they wouldn't even let us in to tour the plant.

On September 1, 1957, a reorganization of the Department of Public Safety was put into effect, setting up six areas with regional commanders, with one company of Rangers to each commander. Then an intelligence outfit was formed in Austin. Regional commanders had simply not had experience in enforcing the law in strike situations. Rangers couldn't move without getting word from regional commanders, and the ideas of the commanders were foreign to the ideas of the Rangers, who had worked strikes before and thought they knew how to handle them. The intelligence people were sent in to infiltrate the union; but the union people spotted them before *God* got the word. Eventually, the Ranger companies were taken out of the jurisdiction of regional commanders and worked directly out of Austin, as they still do.

Lone Star Steel is a hell of a big outfit. When workers were out on strike, they'd look up every morning and see those big smokestacks belching out that reddish-orange dust day in and day out. They knew the plant was going on without them, and it really got to them after a while. In the strikers' minds, the scabs were taking their jobs, taking food out of their families' mouths. They had only a little grocery money. They'd always lived from payday to payday; when the money stopped, there was nothing for the TV set payment, no money for going to the beauty shop, no money to make the car payment or get the car fixed if it needed work. When they thought of those scabs working twelve hours a day and more, getting what should be their money, they'd get very upset, and that was when violence would erupt. The scabs went on overtime after forty hours a week; on weekends, they'd get double overtime. This became very expensive for the plant, too. It would have been economically more feasible for E. B.

Germany to close the plant down, but it was a test of will. He wouldn't close.

Before the strike was over, fences had been cut, houses shot into, people beaten, buildings burned, cattle shot, cars molested (usually by putting sugar in the gas tank and/or breaking the windshields), trucks overturned, and threatening phone calls made. Bombs were used, too, and they did the most serious damage. Among other things, a pipeline was blown up.

The first time the dissatisfied workers tried bombing, sticks of dynamite and cheap alarm clocks were used, with the timing device set by the hour hand so that it wouldn't contact for close to twelve hours. It was thought the bombs were probably planted by confederates of the strikers working inside the plant, who would hide bombs inside the machinery. In November, the same group set dynamite to the gas line they thought fed the plant. Instead, they blew up the gas line that fed the hospitals in the area. After that, public opinion was against them and the strike was settled quickly.

By the time the strike was finally over, we had heard so many false reports that nobody expected the thing ever would be settled. Early one afternoon we got word that the strike had been called off. We were really tired. I was rooming with Lester Robertson; that night we ate and visited and were told that we would be relieved within a couple of days. An announcement was made at the plant that the next morning an employment office in Daingerfield would open and people could come and sign up for their old jobs according to seniority. All strikers except for the walkout leaders would be rehired. The company and the union agreed to arbitration on the fate of the leaders. At 8:00 A.M. the next morning, I got a call that there was big trouble at the employment office. I headed over there and took a bullhorn with me. When I got there, I could see the problem. The people were crowding into the little building with so much force that they were creating a dangerous situation; they were packed so tightly they had already knocked out a plate glass window. Apparently they had understood the arrangement to be a first-come, first-served one; they were so eager to get their jobs back and so frightened they wouldn't that they had panicked.

I pushed and shoved my way up to the front of the crowd and got up on a chair with the bullhorn, hoping to calm them down. Into the horn I said, "Y'all are all pressing too much, and there's no need of it—someone might get hurt. So just think what it would be like if you were all buck naked and pressing like that!" They all slowed it down after that. It was just that they wanted their jobs back so much.

Most of the union's leaders were out of the plant for at least eighteen months; many never returned to work.

The second Lone Star Steel strike I worked began in 1968. At that time, Lone Star Steel had become a subsidiary of Northwest Industries, a Chicago-based multi-holding company. The plant had a lucrative contract to furnish shell casings to the federal government. In 1968, Lone Star boasted a sales volume of more than $100 million per year, employing more than 3,000 people, 1,000 of them non-union. During this strike, ninety-five percent of the workers went out on strike, asking for a "basic steel" contract, as they had had between 1956 and 1958, with provisions for a pension plan, improved benefits, vacations, etc. Wages were not an issue, as Lone Star had kept pace with wage increases across the nation.

During the 1957 strike, work had been so plentiful in that area, because other employers still existed, that strikers could usually go somewhere else for a job. In the 1968 strike, Lone Star Steel had so monopolized the area that there wasn't any-

Strikers at dawn.

Strike in 1968. Rigler on duty with his back to the camera.

where else to go, so the situation caused a lot of pressure, and pressure breeds violence.

When trucks left the plant with steel, whether in roll form or pipe that would become shell casings, they were subject to attack. That part of the country was heavily wooded, with many hills and valleys. Men would hide in those areas and shoot at the trucks' tires or even the gas tanks. By the time the Rangers could get there, the culprits would have fled into the woods. We just didn't have enough men to cover all the problem areas.

One morning close to noon, the phone rang in the mess hall. The caller told the manager, "There's a faded denim jacket in there, and in the pocket is a bomb set to go off at 12:00 noon straight up." Sure enough, we found the bomb and disarmed it, ten minutes before it was set to go off, when some 200 workers would be eating. The device was primitive, but quite dangerous.

At night, we would often hear a bomb go off and not know until the next morning where it had hit. There was a twenty by forty foot building near the plant, used as a real estate office to help find housing for workers; it was blown all to pieces one night. Bombs were placed in the big smokestacks, aimed at blowing them down. More than once, bombs were hidden in the rooms of Rangers or Highway Patrolmen working the strike. Lone Star offered a $5,000 reward for information leading to the arrest of those guilty of bombing, sabotage, arson, or other acts of violence on company property resulting in either damage or personal injury.

People who were working would find their car and truck tires shot when they came out of the plant, or someone would shoot them out as they left. Once Captain Crowder and Ranger Bob Mitchell borrowed a pickup, dressed in work clothes and hard hats, and rode out of the gates. A couple of guys fired on them and shot the tires out. Crowder ran them down and arrested them. We were unable to get a conviction on them, though. When an industry supports an entire section of the state, you are never going to find a jury that will convict this kind of wrongdoer. It becomes a long exercise in frustration.

One day two trucks came from Fort Worth to get steel; one had less than 4,000 miles on it, and the other had only the mileage from Fort Worth. They loaded in the afternoon, but instead of driving out of the area, they stopped at a Holiday Inn in Mt. Pleasant for the night. About 9:00 P.M. that night we got a call that the trucks had been dynamited. The explosion was so strong it bent the pipe they were carrying into L-shapes. We arrested three people within fifteen minutes or so, later managed to get them indicted and had a trial, but we got no conviction. It was the same old story.

Over a period of time, after so many hours under this kind of tension, a man reaches a point that he can never let himself relax. It doesn't matter that he feels he is on the side of the right; never knowing if he might one day be shot, find his room blown up, or be goaded into a fight can be tough to live with for extended periods. The Rangers were living in a hostile environment. They knew if they took any action, they could be hurt, even killed. Most locals didn't even want to be seen talking to them.

I remember the people at Hill's Cafe, adjacent to the Hilltop Motel, because they were among the few people who were nice to us. The motel people could afford to be nice, I suppose—we kept the place at full occupancy—but they took a risk having us there. I always felt they were on our side.

I never fought in a war, but the only difference I can see between a war and a strike situation is that in a strike, the side there to maintain order can't shoot back. The Ranger had to take all the crap without retaliating. This lengthy strike caused many people on both sides to develop health problems. Every day the Rangers hoped that the strike would be settled so they could be back with their families and return to regular Ranger duty. I'm certain that every day the families of those on strike wished for an end to it as well.

Strike situations seem to bring out the worst in people. So many people who supposedly have a high degree of moral character will follow a few people who are totally uncaring for anything except their own purposes. It is a kind of mob craziness—those following will believe anything they are told, and imaginations run wild. The rank and file believe that if one of the strikers' homes burns down, the company is responsible. I would say that less than five percent of those on strike cause ninety-five percent of the trouble, and only ten people can do a great deal of harm when operating under the cover of darkness. During this strike, some of the troublemakers weren't even employees of Lone Star Steel; they just wanted to be sorry bastards. This is strong language, but I can't think of more descriptive words.

The newspapers—Dallas, Longview, Shreveport, Houston, Texarkana, and Tyler—were all over the situation, always out there shooting pictures, interviewing, creating confusion, and stirring up tension. I know they only wanted to get a story, but they added to the chaos.

Many people were hurt physically, beaten up and stabbed. At least 200 people were injured and hospitalized during the course of the long strike. At least four guards were badly injured, two of them having been ambushed in an isolated area of the plant compound. A ten-county area was affected. Almost all violence occurred at night; someone would just jump on a person who was still working and "teach him a lesson." A great deal of the violence was aimed at people who cooperated in any way with the effort to keep the plant open. People who rented houses to workers were threatened, and businesses were persuaded not to sell goods to scabs.

I wasn't on duty the day the man got killed. He was not

among the workers housed at the plant, and he and another man were traveling from home to work, a distance of about six miles. Someone just opened up on him and killed him with one shotgun blast. The man was about twenty-seven years old, with a wife and three children. I helped look for suspects afterwards.

Most of the violence at a general strike will occur when shifts are changing. We were required to work the main gate at every shift change. The change took from twenty-five to thirty minutes. One of the favorite tactics was scattering nails and tacks on the road. The most effective flat producer was called a Russian star; no matter how it landed when thrown, it would puncture any tire. Sometimes we would have four or five flats per week. The water wells were poisoned, fences were cut, cattle were killed, trucks were dynamited, and shots were fired into houses—all during the course of a 210-day strike.

The Rangers started out working twelve to fifteen hours a day, but we were on call at all times. Even when we were off duty, the media wouldn't give us any rest. I worked that strike from October 27, 1968, to May 17, 1969. Between nine and twenty-six of us Rangers worked at a given time, plus between four and forty-six Highway Patrolmen. Morris County had only a sheriff and two deputies.

The worst confrontation I can recall happened at the main gate one cold morning. This main gate was actually a boulevard, a two-sided street with a small island running through the middle. Sunday afternoon about 3:30 I went on duty. About 7:00 P.M. Captain Crowder asked for an all-night volunteer unit. Somehow, Unit 26 (mine) was nominated. There were rumors that something was going to happen the next morning, but no one knew just what. About 3:30 or 4:00 A.M. cars and pickups, hundreds of them, started coming up the road to union headquarters between Lone Star Steel and Daingerfield. Someone came and told me a continuous caravan was planned for the front of the plant to block cars coming to work that morning. We woke Captain Crowder and told him; he called the Highway Patrol in and put them down at the end toward Longview, where a state highway branched off to the right.

Along about 6:15 A.M. the caravan started. When the cars got down to where they planned to make the turn to block the road, the Highway Patrolmen would shove them off on the other road. The shift was due to change at 7:00 A.M., and we knew that would be the most likely time to expect violence. About 6:45 A.M.—I remember that it was very cold, misting, and sleeting a little bit—the strikers started changing pickets. Though they were not supposed to interfere with the ingress of cars, the new pickets tried to get the cars coming in to brush them.

By the time what was about to happen became clear, about ten or fifteen Rangers, four or five deputies, and fifteen Highway Patrolmen had been sent for and were on duty. I asked if there was any way the picket line could be closed down, but it wasn't possible. I believe that now all laws pertaining to picketing have been thrown out. Now if you have a labor strike, it would be awfully hard to keep a plant running. The picket law then said that you had to keep moving, you couldn't mass picket, and you couldn't set up secondary picketing.

Two very rough pickets began causing a lot of trouble. It was decided that I would walk with one of them and another Ranger would walk with the other on the opposite side of the roadway. Mine was a big, tall boy, probably well over six feet tall. When a large pickup truck came through, suddenly I heard a loud noise and my man fell. The pickup had one of those big West Coast mirrors on it, and the mirror had hit that giant of a man and knocked him right out. Suddenly there was great confusion. The crowd came charging across the roadway, 300 to 400 of them, including women and children. They were throwing rocks and bottles, but we got them turned back and carried the guy off.

He turned out not even to be a striker, just a volunteer.

I can still remember a little old guy coming up to me while I was administering to the fallen man and saying, "You know, Mr. Ranger, we're not all of us bad. Some of us hate to see this happen." I could certainly agree with him.

After a while, a panel truck came through and got slammed into by another guy, making a lot of noise. Here came the people across the roadway again. This went on until about 8:15 or 8:30, when the shifts had finished changing. When it was finally over, I went and ate breakfast and returned to the motel. I was exhausted when I finally lay down, but I just couldn't sleep.

To put the whole situation in proper perspective, if that is possible: I certainly did not approve of the acts of violence or the way the strikers went about trying to get what they wanted, but neither did I approve of Lone Star Steel's tactics, because often what the workers were striking over was working conditions rather than money. I didn't care for either side. In fact, I just wanted the damn thing to be over.

By the time I finished that nearly seven-month assignment, my most fervent wish was that I'd never again have to see another picket sign.

⭐ 7

Rangers vs. Prostitutes

A sheriff friend told me once, "Give me a whore or a bootlegger, a cab driver or a pawnbroker, and I can solve any case." But he should have added that that was when the whore was on your side. Some types of crime are just plain tough to work. Prostitution may be the worst. Arresting a prostitute is hard enough; convicting one is just about impossible.

In spite of being on different sides of the law, prostitutes and law enforcement officers have always had a kind of grudging tolerance for each other. Live and let live. Anyhow, trying to close down the many houses of prostitution throughout the state is just a losing proposition. Whorehouses have been around for a long time, and they will surely be here long after I'm gone. Certainly they will in Texas. Most law officers would rather spend their time on serious crimes. Frankly, I've always thought it was a waste of a Ranger's time and talents to go after whores.

Sometimes other people had different ideas about that, ideas not always based upon the highest motives. Many cases I worked on during my thirty years of Ranger service were politically motivated; usually one person, sometimes a few, had some power and decided to use it for their own satisfaction and betterment.

Colonel Homer Garrison, Jr.

More than once the Ranger service became the fall guy, the goat.

One of the most needless, useless, and embarrassing of these involved prostitution and politics. It was a shame that the Rangers were used in the way that they were. When it was over, though, no one said that it had been a wrong decision. We did what we were ordered to do.

In the mid to late 1960s, while Colonel Homer Garrison, Jr., was still living and working, I began to hear of quite a furor brewing over the houses of prostitution which had long been operating in Texarkana, Bowie County, Texas. Someone who had some power with the Department of Public Safety began pressuring to have the houses closed. This person did not live within 180 miles of Texarkana; in fact, the call girls in his own area outnumbered those in Texarkana by thousands. Nevertheless, closing down the houses in the East Texas city became a *cause* something like the Chicken Ranch affair in La Grange, where politics finally came into play and resulted in closing down an institution. In these cases, reason is abandoned early, and what follows is general craziness.

Colonel Garrison managed to hold off taking action for a while, but after his death in 1967, the pressure was doubled. Captain R. A. (Bob) Crowder, Company "B" Commander at the time, vigorously resisted this misuse of Ranger time in his area, so nothing was done about it there for a while longer.

After Captain Crowder retired in 1969, the pressure to close down the Texarkana houses increased. It was no one's fault, really, just a thing whose time had come. The Rangers, with the help of DPS intelligence, narcotics agents, and Texarkana police, embarked upon the great crusade to end prostitution in Texarkana. Can you guess who won?

This was one duty I did not care to be involved in, and I fought it. I dodged the first two or three assignments, always managing to get subpoenaed to court at just the right moment. I hoped I would be able to avoid it indefinitely, but I finally got caught. I think one of my fellow officers may have decided I deserved a part in this war on whores and helped things along a bit. I was told to be in Texarkana one early fall evening without fail.

Now imagine this: My wife Joyce's office was holding a party that evening, and I had to tell her why I couldn't go with her after all. She was less than overjoyed with the assignment, and unhappy over the broken plans. But she also was a little concerned about what her co-workers would make of it. They were a good group, and kidding was a big part of their working relationship. When they spotted a weakness in a colleague, they wouldn't hesitate to go for the jugular.

"What do you want me to tell everybody when they ask

71

about you?" she demanded.

"Oh, just say I've gone to a whorehouse in Texarkana," I offered.

"Very funny," she said, but she didn't laugh.

Driving the 190 miles from Gainesville to Texarkana, I didn't feel too much like laughing myself. I thought of the time and expenses that could certainly have been better spent on several unsolved cases of a major nature that I had. I felt that the years of education, the classroom work, and the real experience were being wasted. The worst was that I sensed the outcome even then. But I drove on.

Several of us met in Texarkana late in the afternoon to get our assignments. The city had five whorehouses. I was paired with Ranger Sergeant Lester Robertson of Company "B," and we set out for a house that had once been a motel. The plan called for me to go in and make the deal, using marked money. Lester was to come in exactly ten minutes after I knocked on the door.

"That's way too much time, Lester," I protested on the way to the house. "Why don't we make it five minutes?"

"No, if I come in after five minutes and you haven't closed the deal yet, then we've lost the case. Ten minutes is better. Trust me, Lewis. Besides, what are you worried about—you're not scared of a little old whorehouse, are you?"

"Damn right I am," I said.

And I was. What a stupid thing, I thought—a fifty-five-year-old man with five daughters and two daughters-in-law, called on by the DPS and the state of Texas to pretend to a whore that he wanted to buy her services. I felt a sense of revulsion at the whole idea of it. I could even see before me the disapproving faces of all the female members of my family. The thing grew and grew in my mind as we drove to the house until I just wanted to bolt and run.

The place was a seedy-looking motel that needed repair most

everywhere. The operators were certainly not looking for a lot of attention.

Lester parked a little distance away from the house and sent me on my way.

"Go get 'em, tiger," he cheered me on.

"Easy for you to say," I muttered. I climbed out of the car, took a deep breath, and started toward the house.

Every impulse in me told me that I should go back, but I couldn't. This was my job, I told myself, nothing more. I breathed in the cool evening air and thought of all the other places I could be, doing pleasant, ordinary things. I'd have given anything to have been on my way to Joyce's office party, even though I hate parties. Suddenly that seemed like a wonderful thing to be doing.

The paint on the place was peeling everywhere, and the yard badly needed mowing. I knocked on the door. No one answered. I went around to the back and knocked on a broken-down screen door, secretly hoping no one would answer there either. An inner door opened, and I became aware I was being looked over pretty carefully, but I couldn't see who was doing the looking. I had rehearsed answers to questions they might ask, but there were none. I guess my dress and demeanor indicated to the madam that I was a regular client of whorehouses. If only she'd known how I was feeling! Finally the door was opened, and I walked in.

The "receiving room," I guess you'd call it, was dimly lit with a floor lamp. A television was going in the corner. As my eyes adjusted to the change, I could see that the room was large and clean, with cheap furniture, a divan and several comfortable-looking chairs. Three girls sat scattered about the room. One was thumbing through a magazine. Another was flipping the channels on the TV. The third glanced at me briefly before she returned to picking at her nails.

I was still standing near the door with the woman I took to be the madam. She was around forty. She had a mass of hair piled on her head; the color would probably have been called "honey blonde" if it had turned out right. Large teased and sprayed curls circled her head, but they looked flattened out, from having been slept on, I guessed. I've always wondered why women wear their hair that way. Her wrapper was a floral print, in shades of pink and rose which made her complexion look florid. Her breasts appeared large but firm beneath the wrapper and were accentuated by the belt tied around her still-slim waist.

"Sit down and make yourself at home," she invited. "It's still early, and things are kinda quiet. The girls and I are glad for the company."

I sat. Then I began looking over the girls, because I figured that's what I'd be doing if I were there for real. They didn't look so much different from anybody else. Two were dressed in flashy-type short dresses, which were in fashion then, and the other had a wrapper on, kind of like the madam's. All of them were wearing quite a bit of makeup, but even with their faces painted up, they looked tired and pretty well bored with what they were doing. The makeup didn't hide the fact that those girls were just kids, either.

"It's sure a pleasant evening," I remarked, stalling. They all agreed, each one adding a brief comment like, "Seems like fall is finally here." I wondered if there might not be something good on TV and they'd just let me sit there and watch for a while and then leave. I turned and looked at the madam.

"You're certainly a fine looking woman, ma'am."

She smiled and fingered her necklace in a way that you had to look at her breasts. "Well, aren't you the fine gentleman," she said. "Too bad I'm not working this evening. But all these girls are."

I looked them over slowly, as I imagined I should.

"Our price is twenty dollars," she said. I nodded. "Do you have any particular girl in mind?"

I looked at them again. They looked so young to be here, not much older than my own teenage daughters.

"Not really," I said. "All three suit me just fine." I paused. "But I do have a fondness for small brunettes." I pointed to the magazine browser. She tossed the magazine aside so quickly it startled me. She got up and headed toward the back of the house.

"That's Barbie," the madam introduced us. The girl had already walked out of earshot. "She'll show you the way."

"Thank you, ma'am," I said. "I see that she will."

Very suddenly, it seemed, I found myself in a room with Barbie. She had a petite figure and huge brown eyes. She could have been in high school enjoying typical teenage experiences. From the look of it, she had had experience, all right.

While I loitered by the door, Barbie walked over to the bed and sat down. She had on a turquoise wrapper. She seemed to be quite thin. She might have been pretty in another setting, but I couldn't make myself think of her that way. I looked around. The bedroom had a double bed, a chest of drawers, a dresser, a closet, and a bath. Like the nearby living room, it was cheaply furnished but clean. I felt terrible. I looked at her and thought about what young girls like her should be doing on a nice evening like this—going to a football game or a dance maybe.

"Have you got the money, honey?" She had a real little girl voice, nasal and thin and tired sounding.

"Sure do," I said, and gave her the marked twenty-dollar bill. Then I started sweating.

Time now became terribly important. Barbie still hadn't begun to undress, but I wasn't surprised. I knew what was coming next. It was common practice for prostitutes to examine (*really* examine) the customer for evidence of sores, etc., before engaging in the business of the night. I knew my time was near. Any feelings I had had for the wrongness of the situation were rapidly giving way to feelings about the wrongness of my being there in the first place and the rightness of my getting out immediately.

Barbie was not stupid. She could see I was stalling.

"What's wrong, honey? Got cold feet?"

"No, sugar. I just need to wash my hands." I fled to the bathroom.

I remember noticing in that room that the towels were very clean, and there was a fresh bar of soap in the dish by the sink. It was Ivory. I remember thinking "99-44/100 percent pure!"

Where in the world was Ranger Robertson? Surely it had been longer than ten minutes. What if someone had found him outside and engaged him in conversation or run him off or something? I could hear Barbie's whining voice through the door.

"Anything wrong in there, honey?"

There was nothing to do but go on out. As I did, the Sergeant walked in. I may have imagined it, but I thought I saw a little grin playing on his lips.

"You're under arrest for solicitation," Robertson said.

Instantly I felt even lousier than before. None of it seemed right. None of it seemed a thing a man should be doing. Least of all a Texas Ranger.

The women weren't angry. They didn't even seem surprised. I apologized to the madam.

"I'm sorry to have to do this, ma'am."

She shrugged. "We all got a job to do."

That's about the way she and the girls seemed to look at it; the arrest was just a minor interruption. There was no swearing or anything ugly. We gave them time to dress, get their purses, and make a phone call before we locked the place up and climbed into the car. Then off we drove to the jail. On the way we exchanged polite conversation.

"You know, Ranger," the madam said, "we're really in the same kind of business when you think about it. We're both trying to please the public in our own way."

"There's something in what you say, ma'am."

"I guess if we had to be arrested tonight," one of the girls spoke up, "we were lucky to have this Ranger do it. He sure knows how to talk to ladies."

"Why, thank you, ma'am."

By the time we got the girls booked, it was still only 8:15 or so. It seemed far later to me, and I was eager to leave town. So even though some of the other arrests were coming in and I knew there would be a gathering for coffee and conversation later, I drove on back to Gainesville, arriving about midnight. I couldn't really explain my eagerness to get home. Maybe it was the feeling that I needed to get back to where things were normal.

When I walked into the house, I felt greatly relieved to be home. Maybe there was even a little excitement about the whole evening and how it had turned out. But I didn't know what I would be facing from Joyce. Normally when I had to work late, she was asleep when I got home. Not this night.

A light was on in the bedroom. The scent of perfume hit me just about the time I reached the bedroom door. The light was on low on the bedside table. Joyce was wearing a black gown and peignoir, favorites of mine.

I moved toward the bed, not quite knowing what to expect. She raised up on the pillow.

"Hi, baby," I said. I hugged her hard. "Boy, am I glad to be home."

After a minute she pulled away and looked at me.

"Honey, you didn't have to *do* anything, did you?"

"No, baby, I sure didn't," I answered, with much emphasis.

I found out the next day that one of my fellow officers, Charley Moore of Dallas, who made arrests at another house, had a little harder time of it. He'd run into a prostitute he'd met before, when she was living with an armed robber in Fort Worth that Charley had arrested. The whore recognized Charley, even remembered his name, and gave him a real hard time.

"Just wait till I tell all those armed robbers, burglars, thieves and killers I know that mean-ass old Ranger Moore has been way off in Texarkana harassing whores!"

I hoped I would never have to go to Texarkana again, but three weeks later I got a call. They wanted me to take on O'Dell's. This was the biggest and fanciest place in Texarkana. No undercover agent had ever gotten through the door.

"You did such a fine job on the other place," my boss said, "we thought maybe you could crack O'Dell's."

"I see," I said. "Will this be the last one?"

"If we crack O'Dell's, I'm sure that will be it, Ranger."

That night I wore an expensive suit, a light green LeBaron with pink and orange threads woven into the fabric, and brown leather loafers with tassels. O'Dell's turned out to be much more selective about their clientele than the house I had visited before. This time I was questioned at the door by a very smart madam.

"Hi, there—now don't you look dandy, sir," she said. "Where ya from?"

"I'm over here all the way from Gainesville, ma'am. Lookin' after some of my oil property."

"Well, how'd you hear about little old O'Dell's?"

"You may not believe this, ma'am, but my shoes have been here before."

"Your shoes, but not you? How come?"

"Well, ma'am, my son goes to East Texas State, and I got a check from the bank that he'd cashed on me in Texarkana for fifty dollars a few weeks back. When I jumped him about it, he told me that the money had been spent very wisely here at O'Dell's. When he went back to school, he forgot his loafers, so I decided to keep them for myself in trade. Then I thought, 'Shoot, why don't I just let those loafers take me back to O'Dell's.' So here I am."

I've been told a hundred times that I just don't look like a lawman; and I can tell a story so well that I sometimes believe it myself. The madam must have, too.

"Won't you please come in, sir," she said.

O'Dell's was a real nice place. It looked just like a residence, with a big fence around it. Inside was a neat living room, a big kitchen with a table, and three or four bedrooms, all also neat and clean. It was easier striking the deal this time. But I still didn't like it much. When I pitched my badge on the bed to identify myself as I made the arrest, the girl got a little upset and spouted some profanity. I think at O'Dell's, the fact that an officer had gained entrance was a blow to their pride. Anyhow, soon the madam, her girls, my partner, and I were on our way to jail.

At the trial, Sergeant Robertson and I look the stand. By this time the powerful people controlling the houses had had enough of this inconvenience. I first realized we were in big trouble when I noticed there were only nine prospective jurors instead of the usual twelve. When the defense brought up this discrepancy, the prosecutor allowed that he didn't plan to strike anyone. All the jurors were males over sixty-five years old.

The state and defense made very brief statements, and the case went to the jury. After three minutes of deliberation—180 seconds—the jury returned a "not guilty" verdict. Next, with the same jury, we tried the madam; this time they took only ninety seconds. Innocent, of course.

When the trial was over, I was just grateful to be finished with that kind of justice. Nothing further was done in Texarkana after that, no more arrests. I feel sure that the houses, madams, and whores are still doing their thing.

A rather painful quip made the rounds after this fiasco: "It appears that they think more of the prostitutes and pimps in Texarkana than they do of the Texas Rangers."

★ 8

Lost—and Never Found

June 1 was a blistering day in Texarkana, one of many to come in that long, hot Texas summer of 1948. The first of June that year marked the beginning of an eleven-month drought, one of the most severe in the history of North and East Texas.

Among other things, Mrs. Hazel Carpenter must have cautioned her only child, Virginia, to mind she didn't get overheated when she put her on the train at Texarkana that afternoon. The young woman was bound for Texas State College for Women at Denton (now Texas Woman's University) and the dormitory room where she would live that summer school session.

Years have passed since twenty-one-year-old Virginia Carpenter boarded that train; and today, the young woman still hasn't reached her dormitory. Her disappearance from the TSCW campus that night in June so long ago has haunted me all these years. About a quarter of a million dollars and countless man hours were spent on the Virginia Carpenter investigation, but we never came close to finding the young woman.

Most of the officers who worked the case have retired; many are deceased. Virginia herself, if she is still alive, would be over sixty years old now; but I still think of her as the attractive young brunette in the pictures her mother gave us. I see Virginia as she was last seen—about five feet four inches tall, weighing 120 pounds, a pretty young woman with brown hair and brown eyes, wearing a green, brown, and white chambray dress, red platform shoes, and a white hat, carrying a red purse, an overnight bag, a cosmetic kit, and a hat box. A newspaper article carrying the story of her disappearance said, "Virginia Carpenter stepped out of a cab and into oblivion." That's just about the way I see her.

Virginia boarded the train in Texarkana at 3:00 P.M. on that Tuesday afternoon and arrived in Denton about 9:00 P.M. She was due to register at TSCW on Wednesday morning. When Virginia got off the train, she was with another summer student she'd met during the trip, Mrs. Marjorie Webster. The two women hailed a taxi driven by Edgar Ray (Jack) Zachary and were taken to the TSCW campus. On the way, Virginia realized she'd forgotten to see about her trunk and would have to go back to the station to check on it. Mrs. Webster offered to go along, but Virginia said it wasn't necessary. The cab driver dropped Mrs. Webster at Fitzgerald dormitory and headed back to the station with Virginia. The coed checked with Mr. Butrill, a railroad employee, and found that the trunk would arrive later. Zachary, the taxi driver, said he would pick up the trunk in the morning and deliver it to the campus. Virginia signed the baggage stub, "Virginia Carpenter, Room 200, Brackenridge Hall," and gave it to Zachary, also paying him for the errand in advance. Zachary drove Virginia back to Brackenridge Hall and got out to help her with her belongings. The cab driver later recalled that two boys, one tall and one short and stocky, in a yellow or cream-colored convertible, hailed Virginia as she got out of the cab in front of the dorm. She walked over to them as if she knew them and said, "Hi, there! What are you doing over here?" She was talking with the boys when Zachary left.

On Friday, June 4, three days after Virginia left home, a boyfriend of hers from Dallas called Hazel Carpenter looking for Virginia. He had been unable to contact her at school, he said, and wanted to know if she was back in Texarkana. Mrs. Carpenter, panic-stricken, telephoned the TSCW dean and asked to have Virginia's record checked. The dean had no record of Virginia's having enrolled. Hazel Carpenter then called the Denton Police Department, and an investigation was begun. Virginia's trunk had been found on the campus grounds near her dormitory and turned in to the dean's office. Inexplicably, the office had not contacted Virginia's mother, waiting instead until she called to reveal the mystery.

On Monday, June 7, I entered the investigation upon the request of Virginia's uncle, Dr. E. C. Dodd, Chief of Police Jack Shepard of Denton, and Sheriff Roy Moore. Many officers from Denton, Bowie County, and Texarkana were already at work on the case searching for the girl and the yellow convertible and interviewing everyone who might have seen Virginia. Search parties were checking country roads, nearby lakes, and storm sewer pipes in the area from Denton County to the Arkansas state line. Considerable construction was underway on the campus, and buildings there were searched. Rangers, FBI agents, sheriff's and police departments throughout North Texas entered the case. Early in the investigation, Chief Shepard and I met and decided to open Virginia's file to any commissioned officer interested in the case. The state spared no expense, giving us a free hand to make phone calls and trips to check out every possible lead.

Jack Zachary, of course, was our prime suspect from the start. About forty-five years old at the time, Zachary was an uneducated man who had been in and out of trouble with the law for years, for petty theft to bootlegging. He was known to abuse his wife and children, but he had never been involved in anything like female molestation. Chief of Police Shepard and I questioned Zachary thoroughly in what was the first of probably fifty interviews. He always swore that everything he told us was the truth. We examined him for scratches, bruises, bites, any evidence of a struggle; he had none. His car was checked for bloodstains or other evidence; none appeared. Zachary said he'd checked out with the cab company after dropping Virginia off and gone home for the night. Both the cab company and his wife corroborated his story.

As other officers entered the case, they would immediately suspect Zachary of foul play and ask to interview him, thinking that maybe they could crack his story. He always came in willingly for questioning. Zachary said he'd picked up Virginia's trunk the morning after he'd dropped her off at the dorm, driven it back to the campus, and left it on the lawn in front of the dorm, not far from the front entrance. It did occur to me that he would have had nothing to gain by picking up the trunk and taking it to the school for her if he had anything to do with her disappearance; still I suspected him.

Meanwhile, the search for Virginia continued. We talked to students, in groups and individually, who might have been out that night and seen something unusual on campus, or who might help us locate the yellow convertible. Finally we found the car, but we hit a dead end there. The convertible belonged to a Grand Prairie boy who was sitting in it that night with a TSCW student. Apparently, the two boys who called out to Virginia did not get out of the convertible after all, but were only walking around it when Zachary saw them. Neither the car's owner nor his girlfriend could provide a good description of the two boys.

As the drought continued, the lakes and tanks in the North Texas area either went dry or became very low. We searched everywhere—lakes, tanks, abandoned wells—but found nothing. Hunters and farmers were asked to be on the alert for evidence of newly dug ground or unusual odors. Virginia's pictures and description were carried in the bulletin of the Department of Public Safety, sent to every State Bureau of Identification, every major city police department, all the protection officers of the major railroad companies, and to all other agencies that could help. A reward of $2,500 was offered by Virginia's friends and relatives for any information leading to her discovery.

On July 8, 1948, I took Jack Zachary to the headquarters of the Department of Public Safety in Austin, Texas, for a polygraph test, to which he agreed readily. This was at a time when there were only two polygraph machines in the whole state. Zachary was placed on the machine and interrogated by Fritz Christian, special investigator for the Director. Christian's report to me stated in part: "The subject E. R. (Jack) Zachary was given seven tests to determine whether or not he was responsible for the disappearance of Virginia Carpenter and whether or not the story he related to you regarding his activities was the truth. From the polygraphic findings it is the opinion of the examiner that E. R. (Jack) Zachary is not responsible for the disappearance of Virginia Carpenter and that the story he related to you regarding his activities on June 1, 1948, was the truth."

Virginia's boyfriend, the young man who had contacted Virginia's mother in Texarkana, was also suspected for some time. He fit the rather flimsy description of the shorter of the two boys given by Jack Zachary. While he was staying in Denton, waiting for news of Virginia, Mrs. Carpenter paid his hotel bills and expenses; apparently, she trusted him completely. Those of us working the case weren't so sure. On June 11, Glenn Langford, Jack Shepard, and I interrogated him for about twelve hours. He said he and Virginia were in love and had discussed marriage. His alibi for the night of June 1 checked out with his employer, his landlady, and others in Dallas he said he'd seen that night. Still, we were so suspicious that we checked his story out five times;

but we could disprove no part of it. His story was weak on several counts, yet we had nothing solid on him.

Friends of Virginia in Texarkana and in Chicago, where we thought for a time she might have gone, were questioned. Virginia was described by many of them as not terribly energetic; she was in school only at her mother's insistence and had no career plans. Some said she followed "the path of least resistance" in her work, her studies, and her personal life.

We also interviewed a former boyfriend of Virginia who attended the University of Arkansas in Fayetteville at the same time as Virginia. He said that during the time he went with Virginia, she did not seem to be getting along with her mother very well. He called Virginia "impulsive," adding that she fell in love very easily, and he believed her capable of running off to get married or leaving home without telling her mother. Virginia's mother confirmed that the two had gone through a difficult time following Virginia's father's death when the girl was fourteen, but that they had been on very good terms for years.

Of course, we received many phone calls and letters from people who said they had information regarding Virginia's whereabouts. The leads took us to cities in Mississippi, New Mexico, Oklahoma, Louisiana, Arkansas, and Illinois, as well as cities and towns throughout our own state.

Mrs. Carpenter engaged the services of a private investigator as the public investigation continued without result. He was an ex-peace officer, and we cooperated with him in every way possible. He was discharged after a short time and other investigators were hired and fired as time passed, but nothing changed. If anything, they muddied the waters for us and made working with Virginia's mother more difficult.

None of Virginia's possessions—the overnight bag, cosmetic case, handbag, hat box, clothing—was ever found. The months stretched to years. Eight years after Virginia's disappearance Jack

Zachary was arrested for the beating and attempted rape of a Grand Prairie woman. The suspicion of his possible involvement in Virginia's disappearance surfaced once more. Zachary was questioned again about Virginia Carpenter, but to no avail. Virginia's mother, who later remarried and moved to Midland, still suspected the cab driver, though I confess I did not after he passed the polygraph exams. "I'm not a psychiatrist," she would say, "but I believe a man can lie enough that it becomes . . ." She didn't finish, but I knew what she was thinking. If you tell a lie enough times, you begin to believe it yourself. Maybe that was the case. After Zachary was questioned and released on the beating and rape charge, Virginia's mother said that she became convinced that nothing would ever be discovered about her daughter.

I felt very sorry for Mrs. Carpenter. The relative of a missing person endures a heartbreaking experience. First there's fear for the loved one, then hope, then anger, then an overwhelming desire to learn once and for all if the person is dead or alive. Finally comes a very sorrowful kind of resignation. Some relatives hold on to hope indefinitely. Most are honest enough to admit they simply can't hold on to a memory forever.

Over the years, the case remained open, and sometimes we would think we might be on to a solution. We questioned and released drifters, weirdos, and even some solid citizens, hoping for a good lead. Each time something seemed promising, my hopes would rise, only to have the lead fall apart. In 1958, some bones were found near Denton, and I sent them off to the DPS lab for study. The report came back indicating the bones were those of a person who had died at the age of forty-five to fifty years. They were definitely not those of Miss Carpenter. In 1960, some skeletal remains were found in East Texas. Upon lab study, they were determined to be the remains of a young white woman about Virginia's height. We were very excited for a time. But the bones turned out to have been dug up from an unmarked grave by a boy needing bones for a science project. No link to the missing coed could be established. Once or twice, people reported that Virginia Carpenter was living next door or down the street from them; but the description never came close to matching that of Virginia.

One tie-in that haunted us, and still does, was the fact that Virginia and her family knew three of the victims of the Texarkana "phantom killer." During a reign of terror that gripped the area during the winter and spring of 1946, five persons were killed, one shot and wounded, and two others severely beaten. The cases

Virginia
Carpenter
as she looked
in 1948

were never solved, and it seemed too strong a coincidence that Virginia knew three of the victims. But Texarkana was a small city back then, and it was not so unusual for the Carpenters to know these people; many Texarkanans did. Still, we couldn't help thinking there could have been some connection.

After my retirement in 1977, I stayed in contact with Virginia's mother, who returned to Texarkana where it all began. There is no hope in my mind that Virginia will be found.

It is different now with these types of disappearances. During the late 1960s and during the Vietnam era, mysterious disappearances of young people grew more common as they dropped out of society. With the exception of a classical kidnapping like that of the Lindbergh baby, or a Patty Hearst-type ordeal, policemen have found there is little that can be done. Now we can only cover the obvious leads, conduct the primary interviews, place the victim's description into the computer, and wait. I've thought so often of those days in 1948 and wondered if I went wrong. Was there a primary witness not interviewed or a clue not pursued? Why did Zachary leave the trunk outside rather than delivering it to Virginia's room? Could the polygraph operator have been wrong? Is there a spot near the campus that holds all the answers?

In the absence of any tangible evidence, I have come to believe that perhaps for some reason no one will ever know, Virginia deliberately left the campus of Texas State College for Women, her relatives and friends, and made a new life for herself. During the years I kept her case open, I came to feel I knew Virginia. I think about her often, even after these thirty-six years, and wonder if she is even now out there somewhere.

Who among us has not had at least one moment of wanting to drop out or "get lost" when things seem unbearable—perhaps because of a job, too many debts, pressures, or maybe a less-than-ideal home life? But most of us either choose to hang on until things get better or, without making any conscious choice, to stay where we are. A few don't do either, but make a third choice—to flee. Virginia Carpenter may have been one of those. A little more than a decade later, a man of my acquaintance might also have made that choice, or he may have been kidnapped or murdered. It has been more than twenty-five years since his disappearance, and still I don't know the truth.

On the morning of September 24, 1958, a Wednesday, Sherman businessman Euclid T. Fant, Jr., left home on Scott Street in Sherman about 8:00 A.M., after reminding his wife Barbara he would be in Dallas on business all day. Dallas was headquarters for the insurance and investment firm Fant represented, and he was working on an important case, he said. Normally, Fant took his and Barbara's three children to school, but he asked his wife to take them that morning so he could get an early start. He would be home for dinner, he said as he left.

Euclid Fant didn't come home for dinner, though—not that night or any other. He simply dropped out of sight.

Fant's wife called the Sherman Police Department the next day and reported her husband missing. The Grayson County Sheriff's Office, headed by my friend and co-worker, Woody Blanton, placed a statewide notice of Fant's disappearance on the police radio network. Searches were begun in the surrounding area. Descriptions of Fant and his car, a 1955 cream-colored Plymouth sedan, were broadcasted widely. I was called in early to help with the investigation.

Our first step was to retrace Fant's movements after he'd left home the morning before wearing a navy blue, lightweight suit, a white shirt, a blue tie with gray flecks, and black shoes. Barbara Fant said her husband had taken no clothing other than what he was wearing, and no toilet articles. Fant was forty-one years old, about five feet eight inches tall, weighed 145 pounds, had gray hair and blue eyes, and wore glasses. Although he usually carried a briefcase on his frequent trips to Dallas, the case was found in his office on the fifth floor of the Merchants and Planters Bank Building.

As he had many times before, Fant cashed a check that morning, for $150, with O. V. Estes, desk clerk at the Grayson Hotel in Sherman. A resident of the hotel, Jack Barrett, owner of the Sherman Piggly-Wiggly grocery store, saw Fant walking across to his car on the street south of the hotel, apparently deep in thought. When Barrett went to his parking space a few minutes later, Fant was sitting in his car in the next space, looking straight ahead. Expecting to speak to him, Barrett glanced over at Fant two or three times during the time required for him to enter his car, start it, and back out. Fant did not look around, and Barrett backed out and drove away without speaking.

A few minutes later, Fant was seen at the United Fund headquarters on the fourth floor of the Merchants and Planters Bank, where he talked with some of the workers he supervised, as he did almost every day. They all said Fant seemed cheerful and in unusually good spirits. About 10:00 A.M. Fant called a friend at Perrin Air Force Base, Captain Bud Humphrey. Fant told Humphrey he was going to Dallas, where he had an appointment with some people at noon. He didn't explain the nature of the business any further.

When we contacted Fant's business associates and acquaintances in Dallas, we found that none of them had seen him that Wednesday.

Fant was in the habit of having his car serviced at Claude Whiteacre's station at Mulberry and Travis Streets in Sherman, just across the street on the corner from the hotel. He had last filled the car there the day before his disappearance, when he'd also gone to Dallas.

During the first few days of the investigation, while searches were being conducted and people questioned, we accumulated as many facts about the man and his habits as we could. In addition to his job as an insurance underwriter, Fant taught two courses in economics at Austin College in Sherman. He had a Masters degree in business administration from Harvard University. He had served as a Major in the Army during World War II. Fant had been married for fifteen years to Barbara Kline Fant. They had three children: Beverly, thirteen; Johnny, eleven; and, Bob, six.

Euclid Fant, Jr., was born into a wealthy family, founders and owners of the Fant Mill & Elevator Company of Sherman, makers of Gladiola Flour. Euclid had one brother, James, nineteen years his senior, who was president of the company. Euclid had worked for a year at the milling operation, but apparently the two brothers did not work well together. In addition to his work in insurance, in teaching, and in the family business, the missing man had spent a year as owner of a radio station, a few years as owner of an auto agency, and several years as part owner of a water treatment company. He was known as a man who lost money in almost all endeavors he undertook.

Fant was an active Presbyterian and a long-time Rotarian. In fact, that's how I knew him; he had been president of the Sherman Rotary Club during the same period of time that I was president of Gainesville Rotary. We had visited often at interclub programs. Fant was a quiet, studious man, a conservative dresser with expensive taste in clothes. He was an avid golfer, an average drinker (bourbon and water was his preference), and he enjoyed good food and travel, but only in airplanes; he hated trains. He was known as a punctual man. Fant was thought to have had some brief trouble with gambling; the manager of a country club in Dallas where Fant had a membership said that he had lost about $2,000 in a game operated there around 1957. Fant had drawn against his inheritance to a certain extent and borrowed money from the family estate to pay off past due bills. At the time of his disappearance, Fant had an overdraft of some $16,000 at the M

& P Bank in Sherman. He had tried recently to borrow $10,000 from several people, including his brother, his doctor, and his pastor.

Mrs. Fant said that she had known nothing about her husband's business from the date of their marriage, had not known of their indebtedness, and had no idea of how much money he made.

On Thursday afternoon, the day after Fant's disappearance, Sheriff Blanton received word that a man answering the general description of Fant had been found in Houston. The man was quickly identified, however; he was not Fant. But Sheriff Blanton used the opportunity to get an alert out for Southeast Texas. Later that same afternoon, Blanton called television stations in Dallas at the request of the family, whose members seemed certain of foul play. Bulletins were placed on the 10:00 P.M. newscasts of several stations. Sheriff Bill Decker of Dallas County took charge of the hunt there. All patrol units in the county began searching parking lots and city streets for Fant's automobile. The DPS radio center in Arlington, which had already alerted stations throughout the state, then put the information on the nationwide teletype system. In addition, the services of the famed Pinkerton Detective Agency were engaged by the family.

By Friday, Mrs. Fant issued a statement saying, "If he's alive, I feel that he is sick—that something just snapped." The Missing Persons Bulletin mentioned the possibility of amnesia.

On Monday afternoon, September 30, 1958, Euclid Fant's abandoned car was found in the Union Terminal's north parking lot on Houston Street in Dallas. Instead of solving the mystery, the discovery only deepened it; for on the center of the front seat was a large bloodstain. All the car's windows were rolled up, and only the driver's side door was locked. The keys were in the ignition; the gas gauge showed empty. The hand-brake was firmly set, a habit of Fant's known by all his friends and relatives.

MISSING PERSON

Euclid Taylor Fant

Seeking information as to whereabouts of person whose picture and description listed below.

MISSING from Sherman, Texas

Since September 24, 1958

Please pass this information on to your local newspaper and radio-TV Station.

DESCRIPTION:

Age 41; Height 5 ft. 8 in.; Wt. 145 lbs. Gray hair parted on left side. Blue eyes, ruddy complexion, crooked teeth; always wears glasses; clean shaven, wears gold band wedding ring; Occupation: Life Insurance Underwriter; part time educator at Austin College, Sherman, Texas. Closely associated with Presbyterian Church. Active in Rotary Club; Past District Governor of District 188. Previous occupations: Automobile agency owner, radio station owner, hobby, golf; married 15 years and is the father of 3 children, Beverly age 13, Johnny age 11, and Bob age 6. Wife's name is Barbara.

Possibly an Amnesia case.

If you are in possession of any information regarding the whereabouts of the above, please communicate with the undersigned.

Notify Mrs. Barbara Fant, Sherman, Texas, or Sheriff Woody Blanton, Sheriff of Grayson County, Texas, Sherman, Texas, or Police Chief Les Tribble, Sherman, Texas.

One of Euclid Fant's sons recently called Lewis Rigler from Florida to ask about the case.

On the right-hand front floorboard was a pair of horn-rimmed glasses, a wallet with an ID and credit cards but no money, a Rotary Club pin which appeared to have been stepped on, a set of keys, and some papers pertaining to Fant's work at Austin College. An insurance rate book lying in the middle of the front seat had blood on and around it. Lying over the rate book and the blood was a *Wall Street Journal* dated Wednesday, the day of Fant's disappearance. It bore an address label with Fant's name and box number, which meant he'd picked it up at the post office before leaving Sherman Wednesday morning. The newspaper, which was yellowed from the sun, had no blood on it, so it must have been placed on the seat after the blood there had dried. There were also two drops of blood on the floor on the driver's side and a small smear of blood on the leather part of the upholstery on the driver's side.

The car had been involved in an accident which had damaged the grille and a headlight. Later, Mrs. Fant viewed the car, and she confirmed that the car had been in a minor accident before her husband disappeared, as the mechanic who regularly serviced the car had also said. But Barbara Fant saw additional damage and felt that the car must have been involved in another accident since she had last seen it.

Workers at the Union Terminal recalled having seen the Fant car parked on the lot since the previous Thursday morning. This was corroborated by rain spots and the considerable dust on the car. The last rain in that part of Dallas was at noon on Friday.

An analysis performed on the blood from the car seat showed that it was type A, Fant's type. A check with the Texas State Optical Company of Sherman showed that the eyeglasses were Fant's prescription. Mrs. Fant told us her husband had only one pair of eyeglasses and had to wear them all the time due to his poor eyesight.

We had a first-class mystery on our hands now. With the probability of violence to Fant an added factor, the case was given top priority.

Also on Monday, September 30, James Fant, brother of the missing man, told police that he had received a call from a friend of Euclid's, the Reverend James Bullock of Jackson, Tennessee, who said that he had seen the missing man in New York on Saturday. Reverend Bullock said he saw a man he thought to be Euclid Fant waiting to enter the Rivoli Theater in New York, where *Around the World in 80 Days* was showing. The minister approached the man at the door, his hand extended in greeting, and when the man didn't respond, he asked, "Aren't you Euclid Fant of Sherman, Texas?"

"No, I'm not," the man replied. Then he excused himself and walked into the theater.

The minister did not know that Euclid Fant was missing until he returned home to Tennessee the same day. We had no luck in tracking Euclid Fant down in New York.

Searches of the area surrounding Sherman and Dallas were increased, repeated, and still nobody. The family ran a personal ad in *Time* magazine, which Fant had always read, asking him to call and let them know he was safe. It brought no reply.

Euclid Fant's wife Barbara gave us one lead we worked hard on for months, even years. Mrs. Fant remembered that before Euclid's disappearance he had periodically received telephone calls, beginning late in 1955, from a man named John Joseph Daly. The calls came from Norwalk, Connecticut, and various places throughout the U. S. When Mrs. Fant questioned her husband about the calls, he was rather vague and indefinite as to the nature of the conversations, saying that Daly was just a casual acquaintance. Since Euclid Fant's disappearance, Mrs. Fant had received several telephone calls from Beverly Hills, California, from the same man she believed, always asking for Euclid. In

December, after Euclid Fant had been missing for almost three months, he received a Christmas card at his post office box signed "John Joseph Daly," with the return address of 100 Lexington Avenue, Norwalk, Connecticut, and the notation, "Please drop me a card."

The Norwalk, Connecticut Police Department was contacted for information pertaining to John Joseph Daly. The police department said that this man had been handled by the department for theft, breaking and entering, theft from a person, using a motor vehicle without the owner's permission, vagrancy, and sodomy. When Daly's mother was contacted in Norwalk, she said that her son had left three or four weeks before, saying he was going to California to look for work. The officers in Norwalk also advised that Daly was believed to be a homosexual.

We located several John Joseph Dalys through police and FBI records, but none seemed to be the right one for a while. Early in February, 1959, the Beverly Hills, California Police Department located and questioned a John Joseph Daly. He denied knowing or having met Euclid Fant, though he admitted he was in New York City during 1955. None of Daly's co-workers recognized the picture of Euclid Fant as anyone they might have seen with Daly.

Finally, in June, 1959, after months of searching and walking into dead ends, John Joseph Daly was found again in Port Arthur, Texas. He was interviewed by the FBI. He had come to the Port Arthur Police Department and asked to be placed in jail, as he was broke and without a place to stay. Daly admitted that in 1955 while he was at Grand Central Station in New York, a man named Euclid T. Fant, Jr., had asked if he'd like to have a drink with him. They spent Saturday night together, visiting many of New York's nightclubs. The next day they were together as well. Then Daly returned to Norwalk, taking with him the name of the lodge in which Fant would be staying while attending a convention in Philadelphia during the next few days. Daly met Fant in Philadelphia Monday afternoon. Fant spent money there, Daly said, "like it was water." Fant offered to set Daly up in an apartment in Dallas, give him $50 a week, and find him a part-time job. He even bought Daly's plane ticket to Dallas, but Daly cashed it in later when he changed his mind about the arrangement. The two parted on Monday night, Daly going back to Norwalk and Fant returning to Dallas. Fant told Daly to contact him at his office or at home if he needed money. Later Daly went to Las Vegas and lost some money; he called Fant, who sent him about $400. Other times Daly would drop Fant hints, like reminding him that his birthday was coming up. Fant would send a card with money enclosed. Daly said he never saw Fant again after their time in Philadelphia. The last time he called Fant, Daly said, Fant refused to send him money because he was angry with him for not coming to Dallas as planned.

Daly admitted knowing Fant was missing; he said his mother told him when he called home that the Norwalk police had been there with a picture of Euclid Fant and said he was missing. Daly said that early in June, 1959, he called Mrs. Fant in Sherman again, asking for money, but she refused. Daly later married, but he and his wife broke up over his drinking.

On September 11, also in 1959, John Joseph Daly was interviewed again, this time back home in Norwalk, Connecticut. The story was just about the same.

We were unable to obtain any information or evidence that would conclusively link Fant and Daly. We had been certain that Daly knew Fant's whereabouts; now we weren't so sure. Another dead end, but this one had taken up a great deal of our time and practically all of our effort. Daly continued living with his mother in Norwalk.

By 1961, Fant's wife had received by trust the $100,000

inheritance from the Fant family estate for the rearing and education of the Fant children.

For years, we continued checking out leads on men who fit the description of Euclid Fant. Once, in 1962, we thought we might have located him in New York's Bellevue Hospital, but the fingerprints didn't match. Periodically, we would get word that Fant was living in California, but we could not locate him or verify the stories. One Sherman man who had been a long-time friend of the family said he saw Fant in Beverly Hills, California. He called out to the man he believed to be Fant, but the man denied that identity and walked away. Some reports put Fant in South America.

The physical evidence we obtained from Fant's car had always pointed to a robbery and murder, but as Sheriff Blanton said, ". . . you can't have a murder without a body, and we just don't have one. I won't believe he's dead until we have that *corpus delecti.*"

For three or four years, Euclid Fant's mysterious disappearance was the top case in North Texas. Finally, after years without a tip or a clue of any kind, most people forgot about Euclid T. Fant, Jr. But I never could. Was he murdered, I wondered, and his body so well concealed it would never be found? Did he choose to go off, seeking anonymity and a release from his enormous debts? The fact that his car was parked at the railroad station baffled me. If he had been seeking escape, why would he choose to travel by train, which he hated? Did he do it for a reason, to throw us off, to get a head start? Was he still alive, with a new identity? Euclid Fant would be over seventy years old now, if he were still alive. I suppose I'll never know the answer to the questions surrounding his disappearance. It's very hard not knowing.

Those Chosen Americans

Like almost everyone else, I've always been fascinated with those very special Americans chosen to live and work in our White House. My very earliest memories of U. S. presidents stem from the World War I days. Living with my parents three miles southeast of Lorena, Texas, in McLennan County, I heard stories of our president and how he was leading us in this great war. Tales of patriotism and bravery circulated, both at home and during monthly visits to my grandmother's house in Lorena. How proud we were that my uncle, W. F. (Lindy) Linville, had volunteered in 1917 for the U. S. Marines—when he was only seventeen!

All Americans took part in this war in one way or another, proud to be serving our country. Women seemed always to be knitting sweaters and scarves and caps to keep our boys warm. The nation responded to the war effort with songs; I can still hear "Over There" and "K-K-K Katie." Such patriotism we had, such hatred for the Kaiser, and such pride for our boys who would make the world safe for democracy! Pictures of President Woodrow Wilson hung in every home, and most felt that he could do no wrong.

Our farm was surrounded on three sides by farms run by

men not even a full generation removed from Germany, and this sometimes made for difficulties. One old German lady who lived not far from us would run out in her yard when one of the few American airplanes flew over, waving her apron, shaking her fist, and hollering, "Buzzards!"

On November 11, 1918, early in the day, we heard of the Armistice. I still don't remember how we got the word—we had no radio, TV, or newspapers, and very few rural telephones—but we knew. My father hitched old Nell, our one-eyed mare, to the buggy on that cold, gray day, and along with my mother and younger brother, we started for Lorena to hear all the news and celebrate. When we were about a mile and a half on our way, my Uncle George, who with his family lived on the same farm, pulled up in his 1916 Model "T" Ford with the curtains up and offered a ride to my mother, brother, and me. My mother and brother got in with Uncle George, but I chose to stay with my father and continued to my grandmother's house in the buggy. That day was a festive occasion; soon Lindy and all the other boys would be home, there would be no more wars, and President Wilson was the biggest hero of them all because our country had won the war!

An early lover of history and current events, I followed the presidencies of both Harding and Coolidge. I remember seeing pictures of Coolidge fishing, and of him decked out in the Indian headdress for which he became so maligned. I can recall stories of the death of his son. Then it was 1929 and Hoover and the Depression. I was fourteen years old, a ninth grader, and along with the majority of the American people, I blamed Hoover for every bit of our troubles. I am sure that he was the most "cussed at and cussed about" of all the twentieth-century presidents.

Then came the election of Franklin Delano Roosevelt, the Democrat we all thought would save the U. S. A. In 1936, I was a second-year soldier in Battery "A," 15th Field Artillery, stationed at San Antonio. We were told that the President was coming to San Antonio and that we were to be part of the guard on the parade route on Commerce Street. We were trucked to the assigned area, and each soldier was assigned to cover six yards on one side of the street. When the presidential car came to within fifty yards of us, we were ordered to turn our backs to the street and observe the crowd and the two-story buildings behind it. I was certain then, and I remain so now, that no amount of protection can help a President if some person is determined to assassinate the man.

Anyway, I did get a good look at Franklin, Eleanor, and Jimmy Roosevelt as they passed—maybe I didn't follow orders too well, but I just had to see that man. He looked just as I thought a president should look. Wearing a white suit and a straw hat, he was sitting in a big convertible sedan with the top down. Secret Servicemen were on the running boards and trotting alongside the car. That was a day to remember.

With the approach of World War II, patriotic songs again became popular. These songs were a big part of World Wars I and II, but I never heard any during Korea and Vietnam—I guess by then wars had lost their popularity.

Roosevelt was such a strong leader that most people were convinced the U. S. could not make it without him, but suddenly he was gone and Truman was the new president. Could he do the job? He didn't look like a president should, surely didn't sound like one, and couldn't seem to act at all like one. How wrong we were on all counts!

On one occasion during Truman's political career, I was assigned (as a Highway Patrolman stationed in Grand Prairie) to help escort Mr. Truman when he came to North American Aviation in Grand Prairie as head of the Truman Senate Investigating Committee. I remember him as very decent and kind. I think the next time I saw him was in 1945 or 1946 when he was in Waco to help dedicate a building on the campus of Baylor University and to receive an honorary degree. My partner, Royce L. Calvert, a native of Hewitt, in McLennan County, and I rode motorcycles down to Waco the day before Mr. Truman's visit. It snowed and sleeted during the night, so we could not use the cycles on the big day.

The task of helping guard the president was usually organized in this way: All the officers were given a briefing by the Secret Service in which we were told the time of arrival, the route, places the president was to stay, and the time of departure. Before the briefing ended, each officer would be given a little tag of some color to wear on the lapel of his coat or shirt so that he could move freely about without having to identify himself. During all briefings the Secret Service agent would stress that this was the tentative plan, subject to change upon the president's whim. Many of the chief executives made so many changes in the plan that it was almost impossible to keep up with them.

At Waco, I saw Tom Connally, U. S. Senator from Marlin, Texas, former Governor Pat Neff, then the head man at Baylor, and President Harry S. Truman, all on the same stage. Now Pat Neff and Tom Connally were orators of the school who needed no electronics to boost their voices, and both were great to hear. Truman followed them, and even though he was not an accomplished speaker, the audience hung on to his every word.

President Eisenhower, as might be expected, was like a trained soldier in his scheduling as in all other matters. Ike was the most predictable of presidents; protecting him was a good assignment, for everything was planned down to the second, and there were no surprises.

Lyndon Johnson, unlike Eisenhower, would not follow any plan. He would plunge into the crowd, without warning, shaking hands, and was never on schedule. I was assigned to him twice while he was vice president, and those assignments guaranteed hard, trying days.

Nixon was in many ways like Johnson, always into the crowds, pressing the flesh. When the Johnson Library at the University of Texas was dedicated, I was present on the second story of a building overlooking the front of the library. We went on duty at 7:00 A.M. and got off at 7:00 P.M. A big barbecue was held in front of the library, and Nixon arrived in a helicopter. Those of us on duty had to endure the aroma of that good Texas barbecue rising to our nostrils without getting a bite all day. All we had to show for our efforts was some very stale coffee.

Once when I was part of the president's protection, I experienced the saddest day of my life in some ways. I have been saddened by the death of a loved one, and there is no sorrow like that; but this was a different kind of sadness—a sadness combined with despair, frustration, and anger. As I have said, no one can protect a president if there is a madman who is determined to do harm to him. Nevertheless, those guarding the man feel at least partially responsible.

Others have told the story of the Kennedy trip to Texas, of the feud between Vice President Johnson and Senator Yarborough, and of the ill feelings between Governor John Connally and Yarborough. They were big men, maybe, but rumor had it that they argued like children over who was to ride in which car in the presidential motorcade.

Many reasons have been given for John Kennedy's visit to Dallas, but it really does not matter why he came, only that he came. He was in Fort Worth the evening before he came to Dallas, but I did not have to work that evening. On November 22, 1963, I left Gainesville at 6:30 in the morning, drove to Dallas, picked up Ranger Ernest Daniel, and we proceeded to our assignment at Market Hall, where we would work under the supervision of a fine Dallas police officer, Captain Stevenson. The day was cool and foggy, with a light mist falling. Later it cleared off and became a beautiful day. There was one nice thing about such assignments I always looked forward to—I could see and visit with many officers I rarely saw, shoot the bull, ask about an old thief, and visit with media people, some of whom I had known for a long time. Most of an assignment like this consisted of waiting for the arrival of the president, and a man would get in a lot of conversation while waiting.

On this day, Captain R. A. Crowder and Ranger Sergeant Lester Robertson had gone to Austin, so we had no superior officer present from Company "B"; ordinarily, this was of no great importance, as most of us were veterans and knew what to do. About 10:00 A.M. we reported to Captain Stevenson, who put us up on the second floor of Market Hall, overlooking the dining area. As I remember, halls ran down away from a catwalk kind of arrangement with offices and display rooms off to each side of the hallway. As soon as I saw this layout, I knew there was no way we could adequately protect the president in this place. I had no way of knowing then that he would never make it there.

Most of the officers I talked to that morning were apprehensive—more so than I had experienced before—that an attempt would be made on Kennedy's life while he was in Texas. We all hoped, first, that we were wrong; second, that it would not happen in the city where we were on duty; and, third, that it would not happen in our assigned area. "Please don't let anything happen here," was probably the sentence most frequently spoken by law officers that day.

As I watched the tables being set up and as time went by, people began coming out of the offices up to the catwalk area, and we could not keep them back. There were just not enough of us for all of them. Most were office people who worked in the building. We did not have ropes or bars to keep them out. One lady who was close to me had a transistor radio, and I told her to stay close. We heard that they had arrived at Love Field, that the sky had suddenly cleared, that the canopy on the presidential limousine had been removed, and that the parade was progressing down toward the triple underpass, a place I know so well, having driven through it many times. Those of us waiting up there listening to that transistor radio could imagine the scene along the parade route. In a way, it seemed that we were moving in slow motion as the huge crowd gathered in Market Hall for the luncheon that was to follow the parade.

I saw many prominent civic leaders—some Democrat, some Republican, blacks, Mexican-Americans—some of every one represented. Dallas was ready to show the president and his party an effective establishment going about its work. Exact timing was important, as everyone knew the president was a busy man, so the luncheon was ready just when he was expected. I watched as the coffee pots and salads were put on the tables, the flags put in place—all for the man everyone was waiting for. Just a short time and he would have been there, and then he would have eaten, spoken, and gone on to Houston or wherever presidents go.

Suddenly the man on the radio started screaming, "Shots have been fired! There is mass confusion at the underpass." In minutes we heard sirens, many of them going right past Market Hall to Parkland Hospital. The 2,500 people below me on the floor of Market Hall knew something was terribly wrong. The sirens and a few transistor radios told the beginning of the sad story. The crowd was restless, unsure—by then the radio was reporting that the president was probably dead and that Connally was near death. Soon a spokesman went to the podium, the same podium where the president was to have stood and spoken, and announced the grave news. People were crying and stumbling about; I saw a large black man grieving, in what seemed to be great pain. People who never knew Kennedy, didn't vote for him, and perhaps didn't care for him, were in shock and great despair, not only for the death of a husband and father and son, but for America as well. As Ranger Daniel and I went to our car, everyone was walking slowly, most not talking at all; cars seemed to be moving in slow motion.

Before heading home for the day, I sought out Captain Crowder, who had flown back to Dallas from Austin when he received the news, for permission to be relieved. When I learned he was at the Dallas Police Department, I left the Sheriff's Office where I'd been working and went there about 7:00 P.M. Before leaving the car to go into the police department, I checked to make sure I had my ID because I was certain the place would be roped off and security would be tight—by then Oswald was in custody. Instead, I was shocked to see that there was *no* security at all. The third floor, where Oswald was being held, was bedlam, tightly packed with people of all kinds. I finally saw Crowder and we managed to get together by edging along a wall. He told me to go home.

In defense of the Dallas Police Department, I must say that they got their man, the right man I believe, very quickly. They were involved in a whole new territory, and the chief was trying to be helpful to the press people there from the world over. They even announced the time for Oswald's removal to the Dallas County Jail—as everyone knows, Oswald never made it.

When I finally arrived home at 11:00 that night, l told my wife that from the time of Herbert Hoover until then I had badmouthed every president, and that I would do it no more. Many things done by Carter, Nixon, Ford, Johnson and Reagan may not have suited me, but I have been in a city where the thing everyone fears happened. It almost happened to Reagan. May it never happen again.

✯ ✯ ✯

Another occasion during which I was allowed to "president watch" was the funeral of that beloved Texan, the Honorable Sam Rayburn of the 4th Congressional District. With all the hoopla and Who's Who listing attached to that occasion, it wound up more closely resembling a circus than a funeral. It has stayed in my memory for two reasons—one, that there were more dignitaries there than I'd ever seen; and, two, that it turned out to be much different from what it should have been.

A native of Bonham, Texas, Mr. Sam was Speaker of the House and for many years one of the most powerful men in the world. He was of great assistance to Presidents Roosevelt, Eisenhower, and Truman, as well as a sponsor, adviser, and friend to Lyndon B. Johnson.

Mr. Sam was single and many thought him a lifelong bachelor, but this was not so. He was married for a short time to a lady who was a native of Valley View, Cooke County, near my home.

Mr. Rayburn was also a close associate of the late Senator Bob Kerr of Oklahoma, and on a few occasions following visits with Kerr, Mr. Sam had me meet him at the Red River north of Gainesville and take him to Sherman or Bonham. Mr. Sam was one of those people who could communicate well with any class of people; he made even strangers feel they'd known him forever. Possibly his best friend was Lee Simmons of Sherman, who handled most of the behind-the-scenes work for Mr. Sam in Grayson County. The late Sheriff C. W. (Woody) Blanton of Grayson County was also friendly with Mr. Sam and would be with him at meetings there, helping Mr. Sam to identify people he may have met once or twice before.

Some two or three years before his death, Mr. Sam contacted Lee Simmons and said that he wished to join a church—not just any church, but a fundamentalist, foot-washing Baptist church. Lee knew a preacher and such a church at Tioga, and with some secrecy Mr. Sam was taken to Tioga, where the elder washed his feet and Mr. Sam became a member.

One day I noticed in the paper that Mr. Sam was ill in Washington, D. C., and not so long afterward that he had been transferred to a Dallas hospital. Soon afterward, I received a call from Company "B" in Dallas requesting my presence in Bonham at 10:00 A.M. the following morning. When I reached Bonham, I was surprised to learn that the occasion was a rehearsal for the funeral of Mr. Sam! Already the television cables had been laid, command headquarters set up, Perrin Field at Sherman prepared for an influx of flights, and seating arrangements made at the church. To the best of my memory, Mr. Sam did not die until two or three weeks later, but we were ready.

Despite his high office and influence, Mr. Sam was truly a down-to-earth fellow, with not much, if any, pomp and ceremony about him. I am sure that he would have much preferred a simple, quiet ceremony with just the home folks there. Such was not to be. The funeral day was more like carnival day.

Early in the day, the famous began arriving by various modes of transportation, with a pecking order definitely in operation. Air Force One brought President John Kennedy and his party to Perrin Air Force Base. Lincoln Continentals for his party had been sent by cargo ship earlier and were ready to go well before he and his entourage arrived. Lyndon Johnson arrived in Air Force Two with his cars having been previously shipped also. Former President Eisenhower left his house at the Masters Golf Course in Augusta, Georgia, and traveled to the nearest Air Force base to catch a four-engine plane to Perrin. Former President Harry Truman got on an old Katy passenger train late in the evening in Kansas City, Missouri, and arrived in Denison, Texas, about 5:00 A.M., where he called an old friend to take him on to Bonham.

I arrived in Bonham at 7:00 in the morning, was met by a fellow officer, and was told I had been assigned to L. B. J.'s party.

About 10:30 A.M. the helicopter with LBJ and his camp arrived at a schoolyard. The crowd was huge. Bonham was crawling with the curious, the working press, the foreign press, TV and radio personnel, and Secret Service agents by the score. A holiday atmosphere pervaded the whole town. At 10:50 A.M. the Kennedy copter arrived at another location, giving the people time to get from one landing site to another, and thus to see all the greats. LBJ went first to visit the Rayburn home on the western city limits of Bonham, where two of Mr. Sam's sisters lived. The services started about 2:00 P.M., and most of the seats were held by those from out of the city, mostly out-of-state dignitaries. For the politician, it was the place to be that day.

I will always remember the scene at the cemetery, with the President (Kennedy), a future president (Johnson), and former Presidents Eisenhower and Truman seated at the graveside.

The elder from the Tioga church, who had washed Mr. Sam's feet and thus initiated him into the ranks of the chosen only a couple of years before, now performed a final service for the man. It was quite well done and something to hear.

Immediately after the funeral, Kennedy and Eisenhower flew out, and Truman took the train back to Kansas at his own expense. Johnson went back to the Rayburn home to visit some more. Finally, at nearly 5:00 P. M., he returned to the helicopter and left. I was more than a little relieved to have finished that assignment. It had been a long, tiring day, but I was glad to have been there. I would say, however, that a lot more people had come to Bonham to see the living than the dead.

Texas Rangers Company B, taken at Ranger Station, Fair Park, Dallas, Texas, 1948—Top, left to right: Ernest Daniel, S. H. Denson, Stewart Stanley, George Roach, Dick Oldham, Jim Geer, E. G. Banks. Bottom, left to right: John Cope, R. L. Badgett, M. T. Gonzaullas, Joe Thompson, Lewis Rigler.

★ 10

Professional vs. Professional

The world of crime, just like any other field of endeavor, has its own hierarchy. Criminals come in many types, and the average crook earns little respect from his contemporaries. Mingling between one class of criminal and another is rather strictly forbidden. In fact, there are some criminals—child molesters, for example—who are scorned by other lawbreakers. Within the penal system, they belong on the bottom rung of the ladder.

The true professional, the one who's extra good at what he does, holds a special place in the hierarchy. Usually he is admired (in a grudging manner) by law enforcement officers as well, if only for the thoroughness and professionalism with which he conducts his business. After all, goodness of character is not a prerequisite for excellence on the job.

The lawman knows about the classes of criminals, from the low, sneaking-type thief to the best safe man, from a shoplifter to a white collar financial man. I have always had a dislike for the messy safe burglar, the child molester, the wife beater, the arsonist, the murderer—especially one for hire, or one who kills during the commission of another crime—and the confidence man preying on old or weak people. But I felt very little animosity toward a real professional who knew the price of apprehension and was willing to pay. In fact, I liked a lot of the criminals better than I did some of their bondsmen and attorneys.

At the top of the list of "professionals" is the safecracker. A cut above all other types of criminals, the safecracker knows his trade—he has to—and is willing to take a risk for the ill-gotten gain. Very few safecrackers are violent men; when they are caught, they know how to play the game. Among the safecrackers I met during my career were former carpenters, plumbers, even race car drivers.

Before night depositories became so widespread, large sums of money were kept in safes in business offices. Many were so old and weak that almost anyone could get into them. Safecrackers used several methods. One was called "knocking the knob and punching the pin"; this worked on older safes. A sledgehammer was used to knock the knob off the safe where the combination was. Then a punch was inserted and hit with a hammer to punch the pin so the door would open. Sometimes a cutting torch was used to cut through the steel. First a small hole was drilled through which water was put into the safe so the money wouldn't be burned up. Sometimes the torch would be obtained right from the premises after another method failed. Machine shops often found their own equipment had been used to rob them.

Another method used in safecracking when other attempts proved unsuccessful was "kidnapping" the safe—removing it to another site. This was also used by professionals if the location of the safe did not permit ample time for getting into it, or by amateurs who needed more time than professionals to crack a safe. In addition, old-time safe men used "kidnapped" safes as a teaching tool for new thieves—on the job training, you might say. "Peeling the safe" was the hard way to get in, using crowbars and hammers, sometimes chisels. The safe would be attacked on the face of one of the corners. Enough beating, hammering, and chiseling, and entry might be made. This was a noisy, tedious method, and often fruitless.

One method requiring a real professional was the use of explosives, specifically nitroglycerine. Small holes were drilled into the safe, nitro implanted, and the device set off with an electric charge. Hauling of nitro to the job was difficult, and the danger existed of too much noise. Before the use of nitro, dynamite was employed. Dynamite also required someone with real knowledge of explosives; you made only one mistake.

Another method that had some short-lived success was the use of a high-powered scope placed in a van and trained on the safe combination inside a building. When the safe was opened during the course of a business day, the combination sequence of numbers was copied down. Then entry would later be made. Merchants soon learned to place their safes out of sight of windows.

Safe burglary gangs were often close-knit groups. Usually there were no less than two on a job, but most of the time at least three, sometimes four or five. A jigger, or lookout, on the outside of the building would sound an alarm to the others if police came near. Later all of the thieves had two-way radios. Another jigger might be inside the building, with two men on the safe. The proceeds were split, with the jigger outside receiving the least, the jigger inside receiving next, the safe experts the most. A person who cased the place but did not participate in the commission of the crime would receive maybe five percent.

Some gangs had up to twenty members, with a leader or co-leaders running the show. That way if some were in jail needing bond money, the others would be out stealing. If one or more went to the penitentiary, the gang kept operating.

Mississippi was a favorite place for the safe gangs to operate. Mississippi did not have a habitual offender law. The state also had conjugal visiting privileges. In addition, some of the officials of counties in Mississippi were not above accepting bribes. I recall well how upset the sheriff of a Mississippi county was when he took $1,800 to allow a Denison, Texas, thief to escape from his jail. The thief made four safe jobs before he left the city and came to Denison with $10,000 for his night's work.

There were gangs that had some principles in that they took good care of their families, did not do any damage to the property other than to the safe, and when caught with sufficient evidence were cooperative. Others were users of narcotics, usually by the needle. When using nitro, safecrackers sometimes required a shot to be able to handle it. Most members of the gangs had a woman, and sometimes she would be prostituting while the burglar was doing his thing. She was especially useful to him while he was in jail, conferring with his lawyer, bringing him food and clothing, and generally doing everything for his welfare.

One gang that caused much trouble was the Anderson-Bradshaw gang, which operated for seventeen or eighteen years out of Denison, Grayson County, Texas. They were an experienced, but sorry lot, with no class at all. I had no respect for them. There must have been seventy-five to one hundred people at times in this gang. They operated almost anywhere in the U. S., but Mississippi was their favorite place. After I got personally acquainted with them, they mostly stayed clear of the counties I worked. As they said, they did not care for my brand of law enforcement.

There was no big problem in apprehending safe burglars. The trouble was that once apprehended, these cagey crooks used the laws of our land to circumvent justice. All of them had lawyers; some of the lawyers were as unscrupulous as the thieves. Immediately after one of the thieves was put in jail, here came the lawyer with bond money. It was not unusual for a thief to be out of jail on thirty or forty cases with bonds up to $500,000. The lawyer's charge for making the bond was usually fifteen to twenty percent or more, plus a fee for appearing in court for all hearings in the thief's behalf. Now you could catch a burglar, say in Nocona, Texas, at 1:00 A.M., and most times by 10:00 A.M. the lawyer would be at the Montague County Jail ready to make his bond. No phone call had been made, and still the lawyer would show up. One thief told me, "I don't go anywhere without telling my lawyer. If I don't call him by 8:00 A.M., then he knows I am in jail." The same thief also said, "I am really working for my lawyer." After safe men were on bond, they continued to work on safes. After all, what's forty cases when compared with ten? Not much worse. When the safecracker was finally brought to trial, a plea bargain might be struck and time in all cases would be concurrent. What a frustrating experience for officers and prosecutors.

Of course, the officers had their little illegal tricks as well. One of these was the "East Texas Merry Go Round." You caught a thief, say, in Collin County, and immediately took him to another county so the lawyer would go to the wrong jail. Then for eight to ten days the thief would be moved to various jails in counties in North and East Texas. Most of the time we needed them in custody until the investigation was completed. Many of these thieves had a narcotics habit, and in eight to ten days you had all the information you needed.

It became a matter of some pride for thieves to brag about being on the East Texas Merry Go Round. I remember one of these fellows who made it from Grayson County to six other counties and cleared up fifty-one jobs. When he got back to Grayson County, he was mistakenly put on the Go Round again; this time he cleared up thirty-four more. Was I involved? I guess the statute of limitations takes care of me, because I was. I make no apologies, for we put a big dent in their operation; however, with the advent of federal courts and rigid enforcement of civil rights, we ceased running the Merry Go Round.

Another blow to the safecracking rings was suffered in 1953 and 1954 when an event later known as the "Beaumont Round

116

Up" occurred. Jefferson County, of which Beaumont is the county seat, had been particularly hard hit by safe burglars. They had a few locally, but the Houston and Dallas gangs did their part in Jefferson County as well. An arrest was made in one of these burglaries, and the judge set a very high bond. Through the efforts of the prosecutors, judges, city police department, and sheriff's office, along with state and federal agency cooperation, many cases were made. The thieves over the state heard about the Round Up in Beaumont and the fact that every thief in custody was spilling his guts. Soon they were all looking for a friendly face to surrender to. This event resulted in substantial prison terms for many of these people. Some got so much time that they could not make appeal bonds and so got picked up by counties with good cases against them and received additional time.

In some smaller cities, say up to 20,000, it was not unusual to have five safe jobs in one night. Imagine how the sheriff and chief of police felt when the angry merchant called and demanded, "Do something!" The place burglarized might have suffered explosive damage, papers would be scattered, furniture overturned, or maybe one of the thieves had had a bowel movement on the floor or urinated in the boss's favorite plant. So the frustration of the businessman was transferred to the lawman.

Such was the mood in North Texas when for a short time a three-man, three-woman gang operated out of Ardmore, Oklahoma. They were a man named Watkins and his wife, a man named Mitchell and his girlfriend (she was a juvenile), and a man named Smith and his wife. Their range was to New Mexico in the west, Arkansas and Louisiana in the east, and all of Texas. Watkins and Mitchell were ex-cons and good safe men, with much experience in entering buildings. Smith knew nothing of safes and was the inside jigger. This bunch could hit from three to five safes in a night and would work four nights out of seven. Their method of operation was like none I'd ever seen. They'd leave Ardmore in

117

three cars and would get together on a little-used road out of the city limits of the town to be worked. Just after dark Mitchell and his girlfriend, accompanied by Watkins and Smith in Mitchell's car, would come into the city. The girlfriend would drop them off at a car dealership. Entry would be made and the safe attacked. If knocking the knob did not work, then the welding torch method was used, with welding equipment belonging to the dealership. The gang members carried no tools, only a roll of canvas to put over the window of the office so the light made by the torch would not be seen. Smith would jigger, and he was one nervous man. He had a bowel movement on every job, and he never left his lookout post. On leaving the dealership, they would take a new or nearly new car and the tools stolen from the dealership. Then they would go on to other places such as feed stores, drug stores, groceries, etc. When all was completed, the stolen vehicle would be driven back to the starting point and left there with the motor running. With this kind of low creature on the prowl, officers were soon calling each other, comparing methods of operation and wishing for a break.

Finally after about five months, we got our break. The gang traveled to Plainview, some distance for them, and rented three motel rooms. A check of the register at the motel showed three Oklahoma licenses. One of these checked out to Watkins. A quick check revealed Watkins was an ex-con and was now associated with Smith and Mitchell. I was called, as I was only forty miles south of Ardmore. At 1:00 A.M. I met the officers from Plainview in Ardmore. A search warrant was obtained for both Watkins' and Mitchell's residences. We were out of our jurisdiction, but the justice of the peace and the sheriff's office were helpful. The search turned up many identifiable items taken in the burglaries—toys, cameras, guns, radios, etc. I was told that the judge who set the bonds would set only a $1,000 bond on each burglary case. I talked to him and he confirmed this policy. I then started calling sheriffs throughout Texas, and they either came in person or wired warrants totaling 654. I will give the judge credit; he stuck with his statement and the subjects were not able to make bond.

Smith and his wife waived extradition and gave statements. Mitchell and Watkins fought extradition but finally were returned to Cooke County. They were tried in various counties, with each receiving twelve years. I think Smith received four years. The women were not prosecuted. I heard later that Smith died of a heart attack while on a burglary job in Oklahoma after his release, and that Mitchell and Watkins went to California after their release.

For all their efforts, after time in court the families had nothing left and were on welfare while the men were in confinement.

One outstanding con man I met and grew to like was a guy called Red. Red, in his forties when we met, had spent most of his life involved in crime, though I felt he could have been successful at most anything. He was a small man, about five feet six inches tall, 145 pounds, a snappy dresser, very clean and neat, with red hair, of course. Red was an articulate man, with a certain class that reflected good rearing. He spoke often of his love for his mother. For a time in the 1920s, he was known as the Banjo King of Texas and played on the stage of the old Orpheum Circuit.

Red was a clever criminal, but even so, he spent much time in prison, starting with a Dallas bank robbery conviction. Red had two personalities: one was that of a gregarious, charming businessman, and the other of a vicious, scheming criminal. For a time in the late 1950s, he ran a liquor store on Ross Avenue in Dallas. The store was in Red's brother-in-law's name because Red could not get a license. Actually, Red sold very little liquor in Dallas. His big business was in running liquor to Oklahoma, which was dry.

I first met Red in 1951 when I was working on the murder case of Dallas gambling kingpin Herbert Noble. Noble, forty-one, was known as "The Cat" because of the many unsuccessful attempts on his life. He was finally blown up by dynamite buried under the roadway as he pulled his car up to his mailbox in South Denton County on August 7, 1951. I remember the date well, as it was my birthday, and some birthday it was. By early afternoon, I had seen three murder victims, the first two near Gainesville at the hands of an irate husband, and the third, Noble, near Grape-vine.

The explosives that killed Herbert Noble tore a hole four feet deep in the roadway in front of his farm home. Noble's body was ripped apart; pieces of flesh and bone were found scattered over an area 200 feet in diameter. His black 1951 Ford sedan was demolished. This was the twelfth known attempt on Noble's life. He once said he lived 1,000 deaths a day, knowing there was a $50,000 price on his head, and he kept his life insurance premiums paid up for his nineteen-year-old daughter, Frieda. I don't know if he did, but he should have carried as much insurance on his family members as he did on himself. Noble's wife had earlier become the victim of another attempt on his life in Dallas, also by explosives, planted in the engine of his car. Many suspects were named, and one or two of them were killed as well. It was a tough time. What established the high price on Noble's head was his falling out with another Dallas gambler over "policy" gambling. Policy is played largely by poor people, who rarely reap any benefit from the game. The operator is the only one who gets rich on policy.

Since I worked Denton County, the murder investigation was mine. I worked with Lieutenant George Butler of the Dallas Police Department. The investigation lasted about a year, involving many hours, many miles, but ultimately no arrests. One of our best suspects was a man named Mac, a good safe burglar who'd been arrested during the Beaumont Round Up. Mac's alibi in the murder case hinged on his being with old Red on a trip from Dallas to Houston to rob a rich black money lender with a safe in his residence. Red was good with guns, and Mac planned to use him, he said, if there was trouble getting into the place. Mac's story was that the safe burglary never took place; when the two reached their destination they found a big crowd outside the home and learned that their man had just died.

Red and Mac were arrested and brought to Beaumont, but we could not make a case on either man. Captain Crowder gave me permission to bring Red back with me. On the way, near Jacksonville, the motor on my Chevrolet Hot Water Six cratered; those of you who remember this car recall that its top speed was about seventy-seven mph, maybe eighty-one going downhill with a tailwind. We limped into Athens about 11:00 at night. Red called his wife, and she drove down and towed us to Dallas. Red and I became friends then and there. I never used him as an informant; I simply didn't ask him any questions after that.

A year or so later, Red was delivering a load of whiskey to Oklahoma in his Cadillac. It was two or three days before Christmas, and there was ice on the road. Just north of Gainesville, Red's car slipped on the ice and he lost control of it. He was not hurt, so he climbed out of the car and began passing out whiskey to motorists driving slowly past the wrecked car, shouting, "Merry Christmas!" as he handed them bottles. He wasn't fast enough, though; the Highway Patrol arrested him and confiscated the car and the remaining whiskey. Red called me from the county jail. The sheriff released Red to me on my promise to guarantee his trial appearance. I took him home with me, and he completely charmed my wife and three sons, who had no idea he was a crook.

Mac, the suspect in the Noble murder case who almost got Red into hot water, was an interesting man as well. A fine race car driver, he was also an excellent safe burglar. Mac had a good personality and was married and had children—not the type of man you'd expect.

After the Beaumont Round Up, I was assigned to take Mac into the counties where he had offenses outstanding against him. Mac would "clean up"—confess to—any job he'd done on the condition he could receive concurrent time. His first conviction resulted in a ten-year sentence, so by agreement he could be tried in any county and really not be any worse off.

I did Mac a favor once in exchange for some information. Mac had a girlfriend, and he was some crazy about her. When I placed him in the Dallas County Jail, he put a proposition to me. If I would arrange for him to spend one night with this girlfriend, he would give me information that would clear up a murder case.

I talked to Captain Crowder about Mac, and he told me to handle it as I saw fit. On a Monday, I picked Mac up at the jail, and let him call his girlfriend and tell her to meet us at a bus station in a small county seat about one hundred miles east of Dallas. It was my intention to rent a motel room for them. I would stay in my car in front of the motel, holding all of their clothes. I took Mac to the sheriff's office in this county seat and told the sheriff what I had in mind. The sheriff had a better idea: there was no one in the jail that night, so he would just lock them up together. There was even a cook stove there so she could cook them a meal. This suited Mac and his girlfriend, so I left them there and went back about a week later. I guess they were a little sick of each other by then; the romance seemed to have cooled. Mac did not say anything about his girlfriend or having her stay with him again. As for his clearing up the murder case for me, the number one suspect was killed two weeks later.

When I transported people like Red and Mac, I always asked, "Do you want to be transported as a man or as a criminal? If you want to be a man, I will put no handcuffs on you. When we go to a cafe to eat, there will be no sign that I am an officer transporting a prisoner." In thirty-six years of law enforcement work, I never had one that I trusted not keep his word. I tried it only with mature people who had already done time. Many times we had good conversations and I felt that most were my friends.

Another man I won't forget was Blackie L., a big man, six feet two inches tall, 215 pounds, with coal black hair and eyes. Blackie was one of the meanest men I ever met, particularly to other criminals. He could not read or write very well and had a slight speech impediment.

The first time I saw Blackie was in 1942, when I arrested him on a traffic violation in Grand Prairie. When Blackie got out of the car, sugar and gasoline ration stamps started tumbling out of the tops of his boots. He must have had thousands of them, all from a burglary of the Cooke County courthouse. Blackie was turned over to federal authorities and I did not see him for a while. But for some reason Blackie took a liking to me that lasted as long as he lived.

One evening as I came out of my office in Gainesville, I saw Blackie and his mother sitting in a car. Blackie had lost his driver's license while he was in the Texas Department of Corrections, and he needed help. The next day I helped him study the driver's manual, and he passed the test.

A short time later I heard that Blackie had begun knocking over illegal games in Fort Worth. His method was simple: he'd walk in and pick up the money off the crap table, then walk out. No one stopped him or reported him; but he became very unpopular with the players and operators.

One day Blackie stopped by Gainesville and we had a talk. I told him I'd heard about his new career and warned him of the danger. "Blackie, you'll surely get killed," I said. He laughed that off and showed me the cowboy boots he was wearing, saying he'd made them while he was in the T.D.C. I admired them—they really were fine—and Blackie started to take them off then and there and make a present of them. I declined his generous offer, but he said, "I'm going to the T.D.C. tomorrow to visit. I'll get me another pair and you can have these. "

The next morning when I picked up the *Fort Worth Star-Telegram,* there on the front page was a picture of my boots on the curb of North Main, with Blackie's feet, legs, body, and head attached to them, lying in the street. Sure enough, old Blackie had raided one too many crap games and would not live to his allotted threescore and ten. A very small, mild-mannered horse trainer had followed Blackie from his last raid, down the stairs, and into the street, where he shot Blackie several times. I'm sure if Blackie lived long enough to think, he was very surprised. He really was a man without fear.

Many times I've seen a family with several children, of whom all but one are able to make it in the world. Despite the same rearing and the same opportunities, that one just goes astray. Such a person was a friend I'll call C. G., the first person I arrested when I came to Gainesville in 1947. C. G. was fourteen years old at the time, and he and another kid, both slight of build but heavily muscled in the upper arms and shoulders, would climb the drain pipes to the top of a building, pry open the skylight, and use a rope to lower themselves into the building. After I caught C. G., he was sent to the state reform school at Gatesville. In the years to follow, I must have handled C. G. twenty times. He was in and out of both state and federal penal institutions, and if he was on the ground thirty days, it was unusual. He was a burglar, thief, armed robber, and just plain dumb. But I really liked C. G. all the same.

The last time I talked to C. G., he had just gotten out of the Arkansas State Penitentiary after doing twelve years on a thirty-year sentence for kidnapping a bank president. C. G.'s partner on the kidnapping had turned state's evidence and gotten three years. C. G. played hard-ass and got thirty. We figured up that out of the years between 1947 and 1980, C. G. had been out of confinement less than two years. C. G. said that if his first confinement had been in the Arkansas State Pen, he would never have been in any more trouble. The Arkansas prison has come under attack for its treatment of prisoners, and rightfully so, I assume. But there's one thing for sure: People who do time there seem not to want to commit another crime, at least in the state of Arkansas.

During the last couple of years, I have visited with C. G. several times. He is now gainfully employed in the Dallas area. This time, he may make it. C. G. is over fifty-years old and looks seventy. His mother spent about twenty years being mad at me because of my arrests of her son. Finally she told me the only real peace she had all those years was when she knew C. G. was locked up.

The one negative observation I've made on professional criminals is that almost all are willing to inform on their accomplices if the right deal is offered them. To take care of Number One is the motto of thieves. Still, I couldn't help admiring them sometimes.

★ 11

In the Line of Duty

There is one thing I never heard discussed by fellow officers during all my time in law enforcement, and that was death—that is, their own death, not by disease or accident but by violence. Officers as a group seem to recognize the possibility, but at the same time each feels that it can't happen to him. I guess that's a good thing, really, because the risk is definitely there, but thinking about it does very little good and may even do some harm.

This feeling of invulnerability that an officer develops for his own peace of mind sometimes extends itself to fellow officers he cares about. He begins to feel that it can't happen to them either. Unfortunately, if a man stays in law enforcement long enough, death can and may well find him or another officer who is also a good friend.

I never thought about dying in the line of duty until January 1977, when I gave notice of my retirement on August 31, 1977. From that day, though, I became rather concerned. I had worked for thirty-five years and five months, and with seven months to go, I wanted to be sure not to become a statistic. And I didn't.

But two things happened to officer friends of mine during

my time with the law which grieved me greatly. Even now, though years have passed, thinking of them brings real sadness.

Kenneth W. Harrison, Texas Highway Patrolman, came to Gainesville in 1962, transferred there from Wellington in West Texas. When he got to this area and saw Interstate 35, it was a different world for Ken. Things were much busier for him than they'd been out in West Texas, but Ken learned fast. He was a fine man—as good morally as any you will meet—and had a lovely wife, two young daughters and one young son. Ken was about thirty-seven when I met him, a fine physical specimen standing well over six feet tall, lean and possessed of that important combination for law officers: a strong desire to enforce the law and a keen sense of humor. He was devoted to family, friends, and to the Department of Public Safety. Ken and I quickly became friends.

On June 8, 1963, a Saturday, I left Gainesville for Denton to see a complainant. My wife Joyce accompanied me, and it was her habit to sit close to me, as we had been married only a few months. We met Ken by himself on Interstate 35, within the city limits of Gainesville, and I remember that he said jokingly over the radio: "Watch it there, Ranger." Just six hours later, he would be shot in the back five times, and death would come within thirty seconds.

I was back home later that night, about 11:30 P.M., when I received the call about Ken's death from Bill Gardner, a Highway Patrol officer. Bill told me that Ken had answered an allpoints bulletin about a car that had run off the road on Interstate 35. Harrison had been closest to the scene and had volunteered to check it out. A few minutes later he had radioed for another unit to meet him at the County Jail to help him with three prisoners he was bringing in. The unit had started for the jail but found Harrison's car crashed into a feed store and the officer dying, hanging halfway out of the driver's seat onto the ground. Arrests had been made at the scene.

First, I wanted to see Ken; I simply couldn't believe that he was dead. I met Bill Gardner at Gainesville Hospital and we went in to see Ken. It is not possible to describe the force of the emotion I felt upon seeing this good man lying dead, with five bullet wounds in his back. We were told by the doctor that he had probably died almost instantly, and for that I was grateful. I thought of our friendship, his fine work, his wife and children, and I felt as angry as I ever have.

Gardner had told me when he called that they thought they had caught the guy who had killed Harrison and that he and a couple of others who were with him were at the Cooke County Jail. The suspect was very loud, shouting that he hated all officers, especially Highway Patrolmen. Fleeing from arrest in Missouri some years before, he had been shot in the leg; it had to be amputated.

I left the hospital and drove to the jail, all the while concentrating on the discipline I'd need to perform the investigation and question and handle a man who had murdered my friend and fellow officer. When I entered the office, several people were there. On the couch was a woman, later identified to me as Dorothy Faye Sanders, thirty-eight, a waitress, and a man, later identified as Jerry Don Anderson, twenty-seven, thought to be the one who had fired the shots. Lying on the floor, apparently unconscious, was another man, later identified as Alton Tosh Baxter, forty-two. All three appeared to have been drinking.

The sheriff asked me to take a statement from the woman, and I look her into his office. Ms. Sanders told me that she had known Anderson for about a month and that they had been together all day on June 8, the previous day (it was now very early on the morning of June 9). In the afternoon of that day, Anderson and Sanders had first eaten and bought some whiskey, she said, and then taken a set of silverware from the home of Anderson's sister in Dallas and pawned it downtown. They had used the money to buy a Rohm Model RC-10, a .22 caliber short revolver, and some shells. They had returned to Anderson's sister's home briefly to look for some money, and when they found none, Anderson had shot the gun off several times inside the house. They then started off about dark for Oklahoma City on Interstate 35 in Anderson's 1955 Dodge sedan. Just south of Gainesville, Sanders said, about 11:00 P.M., Anderson had lost control of the car and they had gone into a ditch. When they could not get the car started, they began walking north on Interstate 35; but they had walked only about 150 yards when a patrol car came up from behind them and the officer told them to get into the car. Sanders had noticed a man asleep in the front seat of the patrol car, so she and Anderson got in the back, with Anderson sitting directly behind Harrison, the patrolman.

The only conversation in the car, she said, was when Anderson asked Harrison to let him call his sister in Oklahoma City; Harrison said no, but there was no unpleasantness between the two, she said, and Harrison was very nice to them. As Harrison turned off I-35 into Gainesville, he used his radio to ask that someone meet him at the County Jail to help him with some prisoners. When Anderson heard this, he pulled the gun out and shot Harrison five times in the back, raising his arm high enough so that none of the shots went into the seat, she remembered. Harrison said only, "Don't, oh, don't," before losing control of the car, which ran into the Farmers Feed Store at Pecan and Weaver Streets. Sanders and Anderson crawled out of the car and Anderson reached in to get Harrison's gun, using it to hit the unconscious man in the front seat in the head "two or three" times. The metal door of the building had been broken in by the impact of the crash, and Sanders and Anderson went into the building and hid.

She took a pint bottle of whiskey and threw it onto a pile of feed sacks. Anderson, who had been hurt in the crash, fell to the floor. With his wooden leg, he couldn't crawl very far. Within only a few minutes, officers had arrived and the three were taken into custody.

Sanders identified Anderson's gun, and then I had her statement witnessed, ordered a postmortem examination on Kenneth Harrison, sent for the County Attorney, and ordered the two cars to be locked and stored. Then I interviewed Anderson, and he immediately admitted killing Harrison. When I asked him if he felt sadness or remorse for taking Ken's life, he replied, "Well, no, I don't feel sad—after all, I didn't know the man. Now if I had known him and liked him, then I might feel sad." When he said this, I thought I might lose control, but just about that time Sheriff C. W. (Woody) Blanton of Sherman, Grayson County, arrived. His being there helped me a lot; we had worked together for thirteen years, and he knew how difficult this was for me. With his help, and that of Cooke County Sheriff O. E. Whisnand and his officers, and County Attorney L. V. Henry and his assistant, Jim Hatcher, we got the investigation into fairly good shape.

Alton Baxter, the man in the front seat, added nothing to our investigation, as he had been too drunk to remember anything. Apparently, Harrison must have arrested him hitchhiking on the highway just a few minutes before coming across the people who murdered him.

The investigation proceeded in a routine manner, with polygraphs substantiating the story. Anderson had a ten-year police record when he was arrested. He had been convicted of a knifing-strangulation murder in Arizona in 1956 and had served approximately six years before his parole. He had also incurred a number of DWI charges over the years. He had been free for only a few months when he killed Harrison, and there was a DWI charge pending against him.

Woody Blanton, Sheriff Grayson County
Inscription reads: "To my best friend: A great law enforcement officer"

After some time, the case was transferred to Tarrant County, where a very fine criminal attorney was appointed to defend Anderson. The trial date was set for November 4. I did not feel good about our case for a couple of reasons. For one, Anderson had received a bloody nose in the automobile accident, and a local newspaper photographer had taken a picture of him before he was treated and given it to the defense lawyer. I knew police brutality would be brought up. For another, I was not sure that the woman would hold up as a witness, and without good testimony from her, we were in trouble.

Shortly before jury selection began in the District Court of Byron Matthews in Fort Worth, two sisters of the defendant approached me and asked to talk in private. I had met them in

132

Gainesville when they came to visit their brother while he was in custody there, and they were good and honest women. They asked if I could use my influence to secure a life sentence for their brother. I truly did not believe that we had a good enough case to get the death penalty; in fact, I feared we might end up with a hung jury. I talked to County Attorney Henry, and after conferring with the Harrison family, we reached an agreement and Anderson took a life sentence. I never heard of him again. He was in truth a killer, and I doubt that he ever changed.

In 1983 Kenneth Harrison's son became a member of the DPS as a Texas State Trooper and is stationed in Sherman, Texas. His name is Kenneth E. Harrison.

Another good friend and co-worker that I lost was Ones Hodges. Ones was elected sheriff of Denton County in 1948 and took office on January 1, 1949. Ones did not have very much experience as an officer, having worked only in the Ford Motor Company in Dallas and for a butane sales company in Denton. But he did have some experience as a deputy sheriff, and he was so anxious to do a good job as sheriff. No one ever wanted to be an effective officer of the law more than Ones.

Seven days after Hodges took office, a mentally disturbed man got a shotgun and walked down the street of Krum, Texas, looking for trouble. He apparently was after a barber who had a shop in Krum. The barber directed a barbershop quartet that the mentally ill man wanted to join, but the man's family had asked the barber not to let him in because they feared he might do something embarrassing while singing. On his way to the barbershop, the disturbed man fired one shot into the backside of a man on the street but did not do him great harm. The barber and one customer saw the man coming, and though the shop did not have a back door, they managed to beat a hasty retreat through the rear window of the shop. The disturbed man entered the shop and took refuge, threatening to hurt anyone who came near.

Sheriff Hodges was called, and when he arrived in Krum, he asked where the troublemaker was and drove directly to the shop. There was a rather steep curb in front of the shop, and as Hodges and his deputy stepped up onto the sidewalk, the mentally ill man fired through the plate glass window. The shot and glass hit Hodges in the face and eyes, and he was blinded.

I was in Montague at the time and immediately went to Krum, but the suspect was already in custody. I went to see Ones in the hospital, and he was in amazingly good spirits, assuring me that he would see again. But his eyesight was permanently gone. He was re-elected sheriff in 1950 and again in 1952; the people loved him and admired him for the sacrifice he had made.

No man wanted more to function as an officer. Sadly, Ones could do very little because of his disability. He traveled with me many miles, sometimes on arrests, sometimes on investigations, sometimes to transport prisoners. For quite a while he wore a gun; finally he was persuaded to give it up. He continued interrogating prisoners, but a man who cannot observe the subtleties of facial expression of the person being questioned is simply not effective.

Hodges never really gave up hope that he could see again. He was a blind man, but he could not live in a blind man's world. In the fall of 1953, he told me that he was going to Maryland to get a seeing-eye dog and be trained to work with him. As Hodges and his new dog got off the plane several weeks later in Fort Worth, the TV cameras were rolling; it was a touching moment, and he was very happy. I saw Ones once more, and he told me that he and the dog were going to be fine. I believed that they might.

On a foggy morning in December 1953, Hodges and the dog were run over and killed by a vehicle driven by a man throwing newspapers. They had been walking in the roadway. That morning Ones' wife had told him of the fog and suggested that he let her call a deputy to come and pick him and the dog up. Hodges had refused, wanting to be independent.

Ones Hodges' death brought to an end a unique experience for me. Few officers have worked with a blind man, and fewer still have worked with a blind sheriff. Ones was a good friend and a courageous man who gave his life as an officer. His eagerness to serve resulted in his blindness; his desire to be independent got him killed.

12

Hamburgers and Beer

Many times I have been asked what one incident stands out most in my mind of all those I encountered while an officer.

I have been at the scene of many tragedies—the destruction of Texas City, Hurricane Carla, several tornadoes, and other disasters. These mass tragedies are difficult and heartbreaking to work, and they certainly linger in the mind long after the clean up job is over.

But the case that made the most lasting impression on me for its bizarre nature happened during a picnic supper. It showed to me just how fragile life can be. It also showed how many circumstances must fall into place in an almost exact manner for some tragedies to occur at all. Sometimes one detail can avert disaster. Other times, that small thing can cause a tragedy. There is a fine line between life and death.

On the morning of May 30, 1967, I was notified that I should go to 1114 Fair Avenue in Gainesville. This was the residence of Robert White, age sixty-eight years, and his wife Celinda, age fifty-seven years. These people were well known to me. They lived only nine blocks from my home in Gainesville.

When I arrived at the house with Captain Rogers of the

Gainesville Police Department and others, we found that Robert and Celinda White were dead inside their home. Also dead in the residence were Mrs. Verna Brannan, age sixty years, also of Gainesville, and Dr. B. F. Hejduk, age sixty-seven years, of Muenster. All appeared to be victims of carbon monoxide poisoning.

I had known the Whites for a long time. For many years, Bob had been a scout for Atlantic Richfield Oil Company. He had been retired for three or four years. Celinda did very fine ceramic work at their home. It was no secret that the Whites were not very compatible as a couple, but there had not seemed to be any immediate difficulty before the incident. The home was an upper middle class dwelling with approximately 1,800 square feet of living space.

Verna Brannan was a widow and a very nice person. I had known her and her husband for eighteen years before his death. Dr. Hejduk, a skilled surgeon who operated in the Gainesville Memorial Hospital, was reported to be an escapee from the Hungarian Freedom Fighters who came to Muenster after his escape and opened a medical practice in Cooke County. Dr. Hejduk was single.

Bob was an ultra-conservative, a man who saw a Communist behind every post. After he got acquainted with Dr. Hejduk, he talked with me about him several times. He was sure that Hejduk's life was in danger, that the Communists would kill him. Hejduk liked a certain kind of imported beer. Bob kept it especially for the doctor, and many times Hejduk came by the White residence after making his evening rounds at the hospital and enjoyed a beer or two with White.

This much is known about that evening: The Whites had invited Verna Brannan and the doctor to their home for dinner on May 29. Bob White was to barbecue hamburgers on the patio just outside the kitchen. Mrs. Brannan arrived at the White home sometime in the early afternoon.

The White's house was equipped with a 120,000 BTU gas furnace, with a thermostat mounted on the wall close to the furnace closet. Sometime after the furnace was installed, a three-ton central cooling system was installed, and it, too, had a thermostat which was mounted on the wall in close proximity to the gas thermostat.

In February or March before the incident, Bob had complained to me that he and his wife were both having headaches. I suggested to him that he should have the heating unit checked immediately. Apparently, he didn't.

The morning of May 29 was cool, and evidently either Bob or Celinda had turned the heat on. Later in the day the air conditioner, which was either already on or was turned on, started to run. Both thermostats were set at seventy-four degrees when we entered the house. This had apparently caused both units to run continuously.

A friend of Mrs. White took a gift to the house at about six o'clock on the evening of the 29th. At that time Celinda was in the den/living room on a couch, thought to be asleep. Verna Brannan was in a bedroom at the opposite end of the house, lying on a bed. She was complaining of a severe headache. Bob White was cooking on the patio, going in and out of the house. He complained to the guest about the condition of the women, saying they must have been drinking too much. (This turned out not to have been true; no alcoholic content was found in the blood of Mrs. Brannan, and only a minute amount was detected in Mrs. White's blood.)

Dr. Hejduk arrived while the friend was still at the house and was told Mrs. Brannan was in the bedroom with a severe headache. He gave her two tablets, probably aspirin or Tylenol. He then left to make his rounds at the Gainesville Hospital, planning to return for dinner after he finished for the day. When the friend left the house, she, too, had a headache.

Nothing further is known of the evening's events. When Dr. Hejduk did not appear for surgery at Gainesville Hospital on May 30 by 8:00 A.M. the following morning, his office and home were called. His office secretary remembered that the doctor was to have had dinner with the Whites on the previous evening.

When the officers and I arrived at the residence, the house was locked. Entry was gained through a window. Celinda White was dead on the couch in the den/living room. Dr. Hejduk and Bob White were also dead, sitting in chairs in the den/living room. A partially consumed bottle of beer was in front of each one on the table. Verna Brannan was dead in the bedroom. All four were fully clothed. In the kitchen sat all the food—the hamburgers were on the plates, ready to serve.

In the home's entrance was a cage with a parakeet in it. The bird was on its back and barely alive when we found it. The cage and bird were taken out on the patio, and the bird revived. The air conditioner and central heal were both running. The heater had run for so long that the varnish on the inside of the furnace closet door was melted and giving off an odor. Blood samples rushed to Dallas revealed that all four had died of carbon monoxide poisoning. The report listed the deaths as "questionable."

A test of the home was conducted by the Lone Star Gas Company on June 6, at the request of the Gainesville Police Department and the Texas Rangers. All conditions were as near the same on that date as we could get them to those on May 29. Here, in part, is the report:

1. The heating unit and cooling unit were equipped with separate thermostats, each of which operated independently of the other, and both could be operated at the same time.
2. The furnace closet did not contain provisions for combustion air.

3. The return air grill to the furnace was in the furnace closet door and when closed did not tightly seal between the furnace area and the return air in the area below the furnace.

4. The cooling coil condensate drain pipe, which extended from the cooling coil located in the attic down beside the furnace, then through the platform on which the furnace was installed, was not properly sealed at the point where it passed through the platform. Since the return air area was under the platform, this opening would allow air from the furnace closet to be drawn into the return to the furnace.

5. Portions of the air filters and furnace walls were wet. This indicated that the condensation from the cooling coil was not draining properly. The insulation around the cooling coil was also wet.

6. Inside the fan and high limit control box was a bare thermostat wire connection.

7. The vent from the furnace, estimated to be six inches in size, was separated approximately three inches with approximately one-fourth of the vent area covered by duct insulation. The point of separation was located in the attic. This test was witnessed.

The furnace had been completely shut off and gas service discontinued after the discovery of the bodies on May 30. Lone Star Gas, which neither installed nor serviced the unit at any time, reconnected the gas, and law enforcement officers gave permission to light the furnace and begin the carbon monoxide tests. No carbon monoxide was present in the house before the furnace was lit. Seven carbon monoxide tests were conducted in various locations after the heater had been running only a few minutes. Carbon monoxide in varying degrees, all significant, was present in the house.

Records at the utility office showed that during the monthly billing period ending May 25, 1967, a total of 1,800 cubic feet of gas was consumed. From the time the meter was read on May 25, 1967, till the time it was turned off on May 30, after the discovery of the bodies, 2,800 cubic feet was consumed. This was an unusual consumption figure for such a short period of time.

Were the deaths of the four people in the White home that evening or early the next morning an accident? No one knows for sure.

Who would have a motive for killing the Whites? Not Verna Brannan or Dr. Hejduk, it seemed. Could somebody have wanted to kill Dr. Hejduk, as Bob White had said so often, and inadvertently killed three others?

I can still recall the eerie scene upon entering the house: the hamburgers set out and ready to be eaten, beer on the table, a picnic-like setting, and four dead people, with not a single mark on them.

It was probably an accident, but we'll never know for sure.

13

A Different Slant

During the late winter and early spring of 1962, I began to hear rumors that something "big" and quite out of the ordinary was about to happen in the Company "B" area. Since Company "B" encompassed thirty counties, and I worked four of them, I was curious about the big event. One thing I knew for sure—whatever the case turned out to be, it would involve long hours and much time spent away from my home station. With most lengthy out-of-town assignments, boredom was the chief distasteful factor. I could only hope for two things: that this "mystery case" would be interesting, and that we would be there only as long as necessary. As it turned out, I was half-right.

Late in April or early in May, Company "B" Captain R. A. Crowder called and directed me to go to a motel in Kilgore. I was told to wear plain clothing so that I could not be identified as a Ranger, to use a fictitious name when I registered (Crowder knew the name I always used), and to stay there until he contacted me. I commented about the secrecy and asked what the deal was, and he said only, "Slant holes," which at the time meant nothing to me. I went to Kilgore as ordered and waited there for seven long days before Ranger Jim Ray of Tyler, who was to head up the investigation, along with Captain Crowder and the rest of Company "B" arrived. Soon the story unfolded.

The slant oil well scandal had been brewing for some time, but it finally started boiling over in 1962. We were looking for holes drilled in areas where there was no oil but slanted to reach into the oil pool and get the oil rightfully belonging to major oil companies. These wells operated under permits issued by the Texas Railroad Commission for relatively shallow holes, from 2,000 to 3,000 feet. After reaching a certain depth, the operator who was drilling this type of well would set a whipstock device (a 12-foot length of pipe whose cross-section looked like a triangle) into the hole to start a slant and eventually penetrate the major pool of oil.

The East Texas oil pool is well-defined, something like a lake of oil underneath the surface. The field was discovered in 1930, and within a few years geologists and many others knew the exact boundaries of the field. The slant oil wells extended from beyond the eastern limits of the established field westward into the prolific Woodbine reservoir.

Through talks with Ranger Ray and others in the area, I learned that it was their opinion the drilling of slant wells had been going on for some fifteen years. It was estimated that as many as 400 deviated wells had been operating, most of them in East Texas. These operations were siphoning off fortunes in oil from the rightful owners of the precious commodity. Under the existing Rule 54, operators had to obtain special permits and fulfill requirements in order to drill directional wells. One of these requirements was the directional survey, which would indicate the degree of deviation from vertical drilling. The violators, however, seemed to be largely ignoring Rule 54.

It is interesting to consider how many people must have had direct or indirect knowledge of the crime. There would be the operator, who would have a permit for a depth of 3,000 feet and would drill to 9,500 feet; the driller on each crew; the rough-necks and other hired hands; the service people; the people who sold and installed pumps; most probably, the public service companies who sold electricity to operate the motors; the geologists in the area; and many others including, in my opinion, employees of the Texas Railroad Commission in the area and, possibly, farther up in their chain of command. There was just no way that all those people could keep such a lucrative secret. It was bound to be uncovered.

Highway Patrolmen on special assignment and investigators with the major oil companies joined the forty-five or fifty Rangers now on the job in the Kilgore area. If the Railroad Commission sent in any of its own investigators, I never saw them, though we used their equipment.

Rumors were many and varied. Some said that the slant hole operators would use violence to keep the suspected wells from being tested; others, that the operators would throw scrap metal into the holes so they could not be tested; others, that they were plugging slant wells with cement; and still others, that the Railroad Commission and its employees were on the payroll of the slant holers.

At that time, the Texas Railroad Commission was headed by Bill Murray, with members Ernest Thompson and Ben Ramsey, former Lieutenant Governor of the state of Texas. Thompson was ill, and Ramsey was relatively new to the Commission. They all took a great deal of heat over the matter, particularly since Murray and Thompson had been members of the Commission as far back as 1948, when reports of slant hole drilling first began circulating.

Our first job was to go to the location where the Railroad Commission was to test a suspected hole, and to preserve the peace. On a very warm and humid Sunday, Ranger Butch Albers and I drew our first assignment. This particular lease had numerous pump jack units on it—some eighteen to twenty, I recall. The pump jacks were of a size that could bring oil up from approximately 2,800 to 3,000 feet. The Railroad Commission arrived with some very poor equipment; I am sure it was at least fifteen or twenty years old, and mostly just worn out. Technicians immediately went to the suspected well, and after three or four days of testing, this well was confirmed to be more than 9,000 feet in depth and length. I guess that's the best way to describe the well, as it was so slanted.

All the other wells on this lease were dummy wells. The electric motors on these dummy wells were running and the pump jacks were going up and down; the wells had everything except a hole. Each completed well in Texas at that time had an allowable limit set by the Railroad Commission. The slanted well, known as "Daddy" or "Big Daddy," produced the allowable limit for all of them; if each well had an allowable limit of thirty barrels per day and there were twenty of them, the "Big Daddy" well produced 600 barrels of oil daily. During this time oil was not produced at 100 percent daily, because too much oil meant lower prices, and the market must be kept stable; so standard wells could not produce to capacity daily. The oil thieves did not let this limitation bother them, though; their ingenuity was boundless, it seemed. They managed to get their slant wells classified as "marginal producers," which were wells that could not produce more than twenty barrels of oil per day. The beautiful part was that marginal wells were not subject to proration as were capacity wells. They were allowed to produce to capacity each day of the month, whereas capacity wells were limited to a certain number of days per month, usually eight days only. If a marginal well could produce nineteen barrels daily, that would mean 570 barrels per month, while a good well producing thirty barrels daily on an eight-day schedule would produce only 240 barrels monthly. Thus the oil thieves could make more money per well than the honest folks! The part that is hardest to believe is that Railroad Commission employees required nothing more than an operator's word to classify any well as marginal.

It has been estimated that using these tactics, more than $1 billion dollars worth of oil was stolen. At that time, with oil valued at approximately five dollars per barrel, the loss was considerably less than the at least $6 billion dollar loss they would have incurred at today's prices.

The weather in East Texas remained hot and humid, the mosquitoes big and hungry, and the Rangers were there to "keep order." I soon learned that the chance of violence was unlikely, that any chance of criminal conviction was even less likely, and that once again the Rangers were being used. The work started out at twelve hours on and twelve hours off, seven days per week. Later we worked eight days straight and were back at home station for six days at a time. That didn't mean that we had six days off—just that we didn't work slant holes for six days.

When I learned that the slant holers met each morning at the local hotel coffee shop for coffee and conversation, I went down and had a look at these suspects (today we would call them actors). To my amazement, I found they did not look or act like your everyday big-time thief. In fact, they were pillars of the community, men who took part in charitable work, served on non-paying boards, and were well-regarded by all—just your good ole average East Texas boys. I even knew some of them, having met them in the Cooke County area when they had visited oil people in my area. Others I had met when I was a guest and speaker for meals at the Petroleum Clubs in Dallas and Tyler. When I saw these men, I knew for sure that I didn't need to worry about trouble. There was never any violence, and so far as I recall, no well was damaged.

Early in the investigation, concern showed plainly on the faces of the slant holers, but soon came that look of quiet confidence, something like the child who gets mud on his hands, knowing mother will wash it away and say only, "Now, don't get muddy again, dear." They actually became something like folk heroes. As we have all seen many times, Americans just plain love an underdog, and with the slant holers they surely had found a great one. The slant holers were smart enough to take advantage of this new undercurrent of something like admiration by raising the cry: "The big boys (major oil companies) are out to get us poor little operators," just as they did in the boom days.

The slant holers really organized quite a successful public relations show, once they saw that the public was largely leaning toward their side. Were they to be punished for producing oil, they asked innocently? After all, they paid state tax on the oil; it must have been legal, as the Railroad Commission itself issued the well permits; the service companies profited from the drilling and producing; more school taxes were paid, weren't they, and taxes from oil production largely supported the schools in this area. The slant holers had found that there would be little, if any, criminal prosecution, any monetary fines would be small, and civil suits were of little concern.

After several weeks, the Ranger complement was cut. Most of the slant holes had been shut off, and only Rangers from Company "B" remained in the area. Straight wells on leases containing slant hole wells were shut down for two years, preventing production of 21,000 barrels of oil daily, which amounted to an annual loss of $23 million. The slanted wells were permanently plugged. By October of 1962, more than 150 slant oil wells had been discovered and shut down.

Eventually, some 150 civil and 163 criminal cases were filed. Five Commission employees were fired or resigned. Though many people appealed for an entirely new Railroad Commission, the Commission emerged virtually intact as an operating board. Not one person ever served a day in the Texas Department of Corrections for any of the charges filed, even though everyone knew that many people participated in the stealing of oil. The penalty for illegally producing oil had been set at $1,000 per day, with a thirty-day maximum. The state of Texas sought between $25 million and $30 million dollars in penalties; when it was all over, they had collected only a little over $1 million dollars. Major companies who sued the slant holers certainly fared no better, as no East Texas jury was interested in finding against the local people, the underdogs. The first two criminal indictments resulted in acquittals, and the stage was set for more. Civil cases were filed and tried in Austin; some of the plaintiffs settled, some left the state, some declared bankruptcy. When it was all finished and the wells had been shut down, the slant hole affair was pretty much forgotten history.

Could I forget? Not ever. So much work—so much deception—so much collusion tends to make one suspect of anything and everything.

Finally getting relieved and returning to Gainesville and Cooke County was wonderful. Even after almost twenty years, I never go by a pumping oil well without asking myself if just maybe that's not a slant hole well.

★ 14

Three Rangers

It was my privilege to know and to work with three very fine Texas Rangers during my years of service. All contributed to my idea of what a Ranger should be, and I wish to remember them here.

ROBERT AUSTIN CROWDER (1901–1972)

Robert Austin Crowder was otherwise known as Bob, Captain, and to his old friends, "Snap." Though I had occasion to call him by all three names, my favorite name for him was another, "Number One Man." Crowder was my friend and co-worker for over thirty years, and for fourteen of those he was my Captain.

Captain Crowder was a true peace officer, one of the most dedicated Rangers I ever knew. More than once, Bob said he wouldn't trade his Ranger job for the presidency of the United States. I believe the Number One Man would have worked for no pay at all.

Why would 1 refer to Bob as a Number One Man? When I entered the Rangers, there were six companies, each with a captain, but with no sergeants. The captain was frequently away due

Robert Austin Crowder (1901–1972)

The inscription reads: "To my good friend L. C. Rigler, with
kindest personal regards. Capt. Bob Crowder, Co "B"
Texas Rangers, Dallas, 4-30-52

to illness, vacation, or assignment; at that time a captain took on investigations just as a Ranger private did. The man who took over for the captain during these absences was called the Number One Man, because the captain and the other Rangers recognized in him that essential quality of leadership.

The Number One Man served as a buffer between the men and the captain, often acting as a one-man grievance committee. Thus the Number One Man was unique—he was efficient only if he could have the ear of the men and also of the captain. Bob Crowder was as good a Number One Man as any that I have known. His sense of responsibility was evident in his definition of a Ranger: "A Ranger is an officer who is able to handle any given situation without definite instructions from his commanding officer or higher authority. This ability must be proven before a man becomes a Ranger." "Snap" had that ability.

I first met Bob in November 1941, while I was still a young recruit of the Department of Public Safety and he was already a Ranger in Company "B." Though I teased him then about barely being able to ride his horse Red, Bob looked like a Ranger. He stood six feet three inches tall, weighed about 200 pounds, and was in many ways a handsome man. Bob had the look that many people associate with being Texan—tall, angular, with a somewhat swarthy, leathery complexion. In some ways, he reminded me of John Wayne, James Arness, and Jimmy Stewart, all rolled into one. Bob looked very good in Western twill and boots and had the shape of head that a three-and-a-quarter inch brim white Western hat just naturally fit.

My head shape resulted in Bob's hanging the nickname "Ned" on me when I had been in Company "B" only a few days. The Captain said I looked like Ned, a funny kid in a hat in his first reader in school. Some people have funny-shaped heads, and just do not look good in Western hats—I am one of those. I early became fond of a hat called a Borsalino, a dressy hat, light

Lewis in his
Borsalino hat.

and soft, that came in several colors. You could mash it and it would still come back to shape. I carried one in the car all the time, and to aggravate Captain Crowder and Captain Gonzaullas, I would put it on when I got out of the car to go into their offices. I confess that with that hat on, the name Ned, after the boy in the first reader, was not a bad one for me. No one else picked up the name, but sometimes when I made a mistake in my paperwork, the Captain would write across the report, "Ned—why?"

Bob was as good at being a Ranger as anyone else, even though he was a fine captain as well. He seemed to retain the ability to be a Ranger private while at the same time being the boss. Easy to know and loyal to friends and co-workers, Crowder was widely known and respected in law enforcement. An outstanding leader of men, he was the type of man others just naturally wanted to follow. He exuded a confidence with which few are gifted, but he was never conceited or pompous with it.

Bob was an East Texan, born on a farm near Minden, in Rusk County, and he lived there until he was about twenty years old. I remember how fond he was of sweet potatoes, poke salad, collard greens, black-eyed peas, cornbread, and other East Texas favorites.

From 1921 to 1924, Bob was in the U. S. Marine Corps. He became an excellent marksman in the Marines and developed a fondness for the Colt .45, which he carried most of the time after that. After leaving the Marines, he settled in Dallas, which was forever to be his favorite place to live, though he was to make many more moves. While he was living there, he met and married Lucille Simmons, who had two small children whom he adopted and helped to raise.

When Bob applied for a job with the Dallas Police Department one morning in 1925, he was asked if he could ride a motorcycle. He said yes. He was hired as a motorcycle officer and asked to report that afternoon. As soon as he left the police department that morning, he told me, Bob borrowed a cycle from a nearby shop and learned to ride it by 3:00 P.M., when he went on duty. He worked at the Dallas Police Department for about five years.

In 1930 Bob was selected as a member of the first class of the Highway Patrol, which had only fifty-one members and was then a part of the Texas Highway Department. Beginning as a motorcycle officer, he rose to the position of senior criminal investigator for the Patrol. The early 1930s were hard times for officers, with Clyde Barrow, Bonnie Parker, Raymond Hamilton, and the like active in the field of crime and receiving a certain amount of voyeuristic support from the public. Legend has it that Bob Crowder once waited six days, unrelieved and unassisted, for Bonnie and Clyde to cross a Red River bridge; it may or may not be true—Bob, never mentioned it—but it made a heck of a good story.

In 1937 Bob was transferred to the Bureau of Intelligence, Department of Public Safety, receiving a Ranger commission. He worked Company "B" until 1947, when he went to Company "C." During his early DPS years he was stationed at Tyler, Lubbock, Dallas, Texarkana, Austin, and Wichita Falls. He was made captain of Company "C" in 1948, upon Captain Manny Gault's death (Gault had been among those men involved in the shootout with Bonnie and Clyde).

Bob's promotion meant a move to Lubbock. He never cared for Lubbock the way he did for Dallas, and in 1951 he transferred back there as captain of Company "B," upon the retirement of Captain M. T. "Lone Wolf" Gonzaullas. There he was instrumental in solving many cases, among them a controversial racial bombing case. In 1955, some eighty belligerent inmates of Rusk State Hospital for the Criminally Insane took a staff member as hostage. Captain Crowder faced them down and managed to secure the hostage's release. He also worked some touchy school integration situations, one in Mansfield in 1956.

Also in 1956, Bob was made Acting Chief of the Texas Rangers and moved to Austin. When the Legislature failed to appropriate funds for this position, he was made major of Region V, Lubbock, under the re-organization plan of the Department of Public Safely. Again he was unhappy away from Dallas, so he took a pay reduction to return to Dallas in 1960 as Company "B" Captain.

When the retirement age for Rangers was lowered in 1969 from seventy to sixty-five years old, Bob was forced into retirement at age sixty eight. It was difficult for him to adjust to the idea that he was no longer to be with the Rangers. The day he turned over Company "B" to his successor, Captain W. D. Wilson, was an emotional one. With tears in his eyes, Bob told Wilson, "I am turning over to you Company 'B' and its men, the finest group of men that I have ever known."

From his retirement until his death in 1972, Bob managed security for a major construction company. In May, 1982, Company "B" Captain Robert Austin Crowder was posthumously installed in the Texas Ranger Hall of Fame at Waco.

Bob and I served in many places and witnessed many events during our years together. Though he was a good, church-going man who could make a fine talk on most any part of the Bible, he also loved to gamble, playing poker, gin rummy, dominoes and "moon," and winning more often than he lost.

One of the things I admired most about Bob was his strength of character and his ability to keep the Rangers out of matters that would only have reflected badly upon them. He had complete confidence in the men who worked for him, and he cared about them and their families as few supervisors do. He simply loved people as much as he loved his job and his life; he was firm, yet kind and flexible. I will always remember the Number One Man.

THOMAS RUFUS HICKMAN (1886–1962)

The name of Captain Tom Hickman is surely one that will always be remembered in the Rangers' history.

It was not my pleasure to be acquainted with Tom Hickman while he was an active Ranger; I first met him in 1942, shortly after he became head of security for the Gulf Oil Pipe Line, a part of Gulf Oil Company. It was in October of 1947 in Gainesville (his home) that I really got to know him. For the next fifteen years I enjoyed a close personal relationship with Tom and probably knew him better than anyone else.

Tom was born in northwest Cooke County. The way he told

the story—and after all, it was his story—the morning he was born, a white man named Tom and an Indian named Rufus came by his home, and for want of a better name, his father named him Thomas Rufus.

Tom was a fire marshal and deputy constable in Gainesville. He was always enamored of guns and became a very fine marksman. He played on the town football team and told of catching a train with the team to Krum, Texas, seven miles west of Denton. The Denton team met Tom's team there with wagons and took them into Denton where the Gainesville team defeated the Denton team, had a fight, and were forced to walk back to Krum.

In 1919 Tom was appointed a Ranger by Governor William Hobby and assigned to a Ranger company at Marfa, Texas. Two years later he became a captain and went to Austin. He later served in Wichita Falls, Denison, and Fort Worth. He worked long hours in the Oklahoma boundary dispute and was famous for many encounters with bank robbers. Tom was active in the tough oil boom towns of Borger, Eastland, Cisco, Mexia, and to a lesser extent, in the East Texas oil boom towns, gaining a fine international reputation for the way he maintained law and order.

Tom often downplayed his peacekeeping role, which was his strong suit, by saying, "I always tried to talk my way out of a situation instead of having to shoot my way out."

Tom was another perfect example of how a Ranger should look. He stood six feet tall, very erect, sat a horse better than most, and wore clothes nicely. The Rangers of Tom's time were known for their ability to quiet tough situations and to act quickly—not especially for sharp criminal investigative abilities. The methods used in the boom towns could not be used today; however, Tom and the Rangers of his time added much to the folklore of the Rangers. Until the Department of Public Safety was founded in 1935, the Rangers were under the Adjutant General's Office, and the Adjutant General was appointed by the

Thomas Rufus Hickman (1886–1962)

Governor, so a Ranger's tenure was not at all stable. During the terms of controversial Governor Miriam A. (Ma) Ferguson, certainly not the Rangers' finest hours, Tom, along with many others, was forced to resign from the Ranger service, but he re-entered the Rangers later and enjoyed a second career.

One thing Tom told every Ranger who worked for him was that he did not allow drinking, gambling, or woman-chasing in his men. Captain Hickman usually rented a large house in the town where he headquartered and rented rooms to the Rangers who worked for him and their wives. Then he hired a cook and charged a flat rate for the room and meals. So strong an impression did Captain Tom make on his men that not one of them would take an alcoholic drink in his presence, even years after he ceased to be a Ranger. I remember one time Tom and I, along with Sheriff Woody Blanton and Lee Simmons, drove up to a cabin on Lake Bridgeport where three officers were standing next to a woodpile having a drink out of a fifth. When one of the Rangers who had worked for Hickman saw us, he threw the bottle into the woodpile and broke it. Tom did not see this, but I did. As Tom and the others went into the cabin, one of the fellows asked the Ranger what the hell he broke the only bottle they had for, and the man replied, "That was the Captain, and I could not let him see me with whiskey."

When in 1922 Tom married, he and his new bride and two or three other Rangers and their wives went to an area in West Texas. Tom was scheduled to go to Europe as a rodeo judge in 1923; recognized as one of the top rodeo judges of his time, he worked many of the major rodeos in the U. S. and abroad. Shortly before Tom and his wife's departure for Europe, she was killed when the short-barreled rifle she was packing discharged. Her grave is in Gainesville.

In 1933, Tom married Tina Knight, who was raised in Cooke County. Tina was about eighteen years younger than Tom; she had lived on Hickman land as a child, and Tom said he had rocked her to sleep when she was a baby. Tina had a good sense of humor, and I guess she had to, as Tom was quite the dominant person in the marriage. To this marriage were born Tom Hickman, Jr. and David Hickman.

Tom was forced to resign from the Rangers once more in 1935, during the term of Governor Jimmy Allred. Tom was captain of Company "B" in Fort Worth at the time. It was rumored that Tom's forced resignation was a disciplinary action over the operation of the "Top of the Hill," a famous gaming house near Arlington. Tom always said he was framed, and I do know that the gaming house continued to operate until 1947, when it was finally closed by Company "B" Texas Rangers in a raid headed by Captain M. T. Gonzaullas in which I participated. Tom then returned to Gainesville and worked for a short time as a deputy sheriff. He bought a small farm south of Gainesville and lived there until his death. Captain Hickman ultimately put together 1,500 acres of fine grass land in northwest Cooke County, usually keeping it rented out for cash. Tom cared about soil improvement and was always sure that his land was not being overgrazed

Tom Hickman had more personalities than any man I have ever known. He could be in deep depression at times, highly elated at others, generous at times and quite frugal at others. He was probably worth $500,000 at his death, but in some ways it might just as well have been 500,000 rocks, because he would not spend it.

In 1954 I fell off a Shetland pony and broke my wrist. Captain Hickman hung the name "The Shetland Pony Ranger" on me, a name which became known to friends and associates, many of whom still call me Ranger. Also, since I didn't dress in the traditional Ranger western garb, he hung the name of "Jelly Bean Ranger" on me.

Tom was an avid reader of Western books and articles, and

he had a long association with Tom Mix and Will Rogers. Some people said that Tom was born 100 years too late, and he tended to agree with them.

Tom was very fond of *The Dallas Morning News.* While in Europe with a rodeo, he sent a story each day to the *News,* which printed it with his byline. He was a close friend of the late Ted Dealey and of Frank X. Tolbert, a *News* writer. Each day, no matter where he was, Tom bought the paper; however, he never read it until evening. At home after the evening meal, he would put on his robe and slippers and get in his favorite chair to read the *News.* He started on page one, and if the first story was continued on another page, he turned to it and finished it before even glancing at anything else. Tom bought the *News* each morning at the desk of the Turner Hotel in Gainesville, and he always counted down three and took the fourth paper. One morning I saw him coming at a distance, and I took all of the paper (the fourth one) except the front page and the back page and filled it with the *Christian Science Monitor.* That night, Tina said, I really got a cursing when Tom turned to follow a story from page one.

Tom truly loved publicity; he was his own press agent, and a good one. In 1951 he was the parade marshal for the circus roundup parade in Gainesville, always a big event. Tom was on his horse, and as parade chairman of the event, I was close by. Several news photographers were on the scene, and Tom kept getting on and off the horse, posing for them. All finally left except one poor fellow from the *Fort Worth Star-Telegram,* and still Tom was posing. Finally the guy whispered to me, "I am out of film." I told him, "Just keep snapping the camera and keep him happy until the parade starts at 4:00 P.M."

In the last years of his life, Tom rode the Salt Grass Trail in South Texas, using a riding horse and a pack horse. Once he rode the Chisholm Trail to Caldwell, Kansas. At the age of seventy, Tom saddled up at Gaines Crossing on the Red River and made the 125-mile ride on the Chisholm to the Southwestern Exposition and Fat Stock Show in Fort Worth. Once, before beginning a ride, the captain called a news conference and had a cookout breakfast at his home. The Dallas and Fort Worth news media were invited; they all came, and he did have one great time. Commenting on the attention his journeys earned him, the captain said, "The women all waved at me, the dogs barked at me, and the men laughed at me."

Governor Alan Shivers appointed Tom to the DPS Commission in 1957 for a six-year term. He served as Chairman of the Commission from 1961 to the time of his death. Tom was not a forceful commissioner, but he was a stabilizing influence on the commission. He was a great admirer of Colonel Homer Garrison and thought he could do no wrong, and since the Colonel was a dedicated original member of the DPS, this worked well. Tom showed absolutely no favoritism to the Rangers as a commissioner.

About 1960, Tom began to complain of a pain in his ribcage. I was due to be at the DPS Academy for two days, so I took him to Scott & White Hospital, where he stayed for two days and nights. On the morning of his discharge, I drove into Temple about 10:00 in the morning and went to the hospital. Tom greeted me with, "I told the doctors that I didn't want to talk to them until Lewis got here." When they came, the doctors told Tom he had cancer of the prostate and that the treatment was castration and taking female hormones. On the way home, Tom was quite jubilant and said that he would get a leather sack and carry his testicles in his pocket so nobody could say Tom Hickman had no balls.

Later Tom went back to Scott & White and had the operation. He did very well, but after a short while he quit taking the hormones because of their side effects. He slowly lost ground and was in great pain the last six months of his life. I sat with

Captain Tom the last night of his life. He died just at sunup, with only Tina and me there. As we had a cup of coffee, waiting for the funeral home people, I told Tina, "For fifteen years I have known this unique man. He stood for law and order. He was a man who never spoke out of both sides of his mouth. I always liked being with him. He was a great practical joker who enjoyed a joke on himself as much as he liked playing them on others. I will miss him very much."

And I do.

MANUEL T. (LONE WOLF) GONZAULLAS (1891–1977)

From 1947 until 1951, I had the good fortune to work under the command of Captain M. T. (Lone Wolf) Gonzaullas, and I never have had a more pleasant four years. There are so many myths about this man that it is a pleasure to dispel some of them. During his years of service to the Texas Rangers, "Lone Wolf" became a legendary name. In May 1982, Captain M. T. Gonzaullas was installed in the Texas Ranger Hall of Fame at Waco.

No one ever got really close to "Lone Wolf," unless it was his wife Laura. No one knew exactly where he was born or anything much about his life before he enlisted in the Ranger service about 1921. My good friend Captain Tom Hickman knew M. T. about as well as anyone, and he said that he enlisted "Lone Wolf" twice in the Ranger service. The first time, M. T. said that he was born in Spain; the second, he reported his birth place as Port of Spain, Trinidad. Once in talking about Galveston, Gonzaullas told me with tears in his eyes that when he was a small child, his family was lost in the Galveston hurricane and flood while he was away visiting a friend. Since Gonzaullas was born in 1891, this would have made him about nine at the time. I tend to believe this story.

162

In 1920, M. T. and Laura were running a small cafe in Wichita Falls that the Rangers frequented. They liked M. T. so much that they enlisted him in the service, so the story goes. A second version of his enlistment gives the location of the cafe as El Paso. The name "Lone Wolf" came from his years of service to the Treasury Department in the 1920s as an undercover agent. Evidently, M. T. preferred to work alone, and from that he got the name, which did not fit him at all as a Ranger.

In 1947 I worked for two months at the Dallas office in the old Ranger building at Fair Park. I was a new Ranger, and Captain Gonzaullas wanted me to study the report forms and learn some Ranger policies before going out into the field. I was also waiting to be assigned a car before heading for Gainesville. I can still remember the morning I left for my assignment. M. T. followed me out to the car and said, "Now, Lewis, I picked you to be a Ranger in Company "B" because you have the intelligence to be a fine officer, and you can take care of those six counties (Cooke, Wise, Montague, Grayson, Denton, and Collin) without help. Don't be calling me with little problems. Call me if you have to shoot anyone. Be sure I can find you in case of emergency. Goodbye."

Well, about three weeks later I thought I had a real problem, so at 7:00 A.M. one morning I went to the Dallas office and walked up to the Captain's desk. He was preoccupied and only nodded, so I waited a minute, then said, "Captain, I have a problem." He exploded, yelling, "Now, by God, I told you to take care of the problems yourself. Now get out of here and go do it." During my last thirty years of Ranger service I never had a problem I felt I couldn't handle, and M. T. got the credit for my independence.

M. T. worked in the Rangers on three separate occasions that I know of. Like many other Rangers, he left (twice) during Miriam A. Ferguson's controversial terms as Governor of Texas. Once M. T. ran for sheriff in Gregg County and was defeated. In

Manuel T. (Lone Wolf) Gonzaullas (1891–1977)

1940 he became Captain of Company "B" Texas Rangers, head-quartered in Dallas, and served there until his retirement in 1951. He was head of the Criminal Investigation Service and Laboratory of the Department of Public Safety in Austin in the late 1930s. Gonzaullas later served as technical advisor for a TV program called "Tales of the Texas Rangers," which made him some money, though it was not much of a hit in the U. S. It did well in other countries.

Gonzaullas was not a big man, no more than five feet nine inches tall and weighing about 160 or 170 pounds. He did every-thing he could to look taller—wore vertically striped suits, high-heeled boots, and a tall hat—even wore his hair quite long on top. He was by nature a very cunning and savvy individual, but emotional and caring as well.

To call Gonzaullas educated in the sense of years of school would certainly not be true, but in many ways he was one of the most educated of men. He could write an outstanding report, a skill possessed by very few; and though he was a poor speller, a dictionary was of more importance to him than a gun.

M. T. always referred to those of us who had worked for him in Company "B" as his "boys." He had no children and no close family besides Laura, and we were family to him. We never had more than two company meetings a year; he believed that if you could read you could follow instructions sent by mail, and anything more was a waste of time. Our company meetings were never over an hour long and were always followed by his buying our lunch at the country club.

M. T. always believed that if you were going to do a job well, you must be prepared with plenty of men and equipment. In 1946 there was a strike at a textile mill in Corsicana. About four Rangers and ten Highway Patrolmen were on the scene the day before the strike was scheduled. Trouble was expected and in-deed did come. I was there on special assignment with the Department of Public Safety, and it was then that I began to admire M. T.'s tactics as a lawman.

One afternoon early in that assignment I went with M. T. to a barbershop in Corsicana for a shave. He was all decked out in his Ranger Rig—a big diamond on his finger and another in a stickpin, with matching gold engraved .45 automatic guns. When the barber started to lay the chair back, M. T. said, "No, shave me sitting up." Immediately the word spread that Gonzaullas was in the city and that he had been in so many gunfights that he must ever be alert. The next week I took him to his regular barbershop at the Adolphus Hotel in Dallas, where he was laid back and shaved while a good-looking lady manicured his nails and a shine man did his shoes. Apparently, his image was already established there in Dallas.

I have heard that M. T. was responsible for the deaths of anywhere from thirty to thirty-nine men. Nothing could be further from the truth. So far as I know, he killed three men, all in the line of duty.

In 1920, while on duty in the oilfield areas of Eastland, Cisco, Desdemona, and Ranger, M. T. killed a man. With M. T. was Martin Koonsman, another Ranger, and both were placed in the county jail at Eastland and held without bond. I believe that the date of their jailing was November 20, 1920. Tom Hickman told me that he delivered their paychecks to them while they were in jail. A few days later the sheriff, feeling the pressure from Rangers in the area, citizens, and the attorney general, released the men and they were no-billed on December 14, 1920, by the grand jury. M. T. told me that it gave him a good deal of satisfaction when he later put the sheriff in his own jail in Eastland on a felony charge.

The second Gonzaullas victim was a man "Lone Wolf" was serving a federal warrant against in Beaumont in the early 1920s. Under the law at that time, "Lone Wolf" was to be tried in federal court and defended by a lawyer of the federal government. His trial was held in Sherman, and his lawyer was Randolph Bryant, then a young assistant district attorney and later a federal judge in the Eastern Judicial District. "Lone Wolf" was found not guilty.

In about 1946 Gonzaullas killed the third man in Longview and was no-billed by the Gregg County grand jury. This death was in self-defense, as the man fired first, putting a hole in Gonzaullas' coat. As with other officers, Gonzaullas never was one to dwell on these instances, seeing them as only part of his job—unfortunate, perhaps, but necessary.

Since Gonzaullas did not drink, he was never caught with his guard down. He had more charisma than any man I ever knew. Though he avoided publicity, it followed him everywhere. Even to the day of his death some twenty-six years after he left the Ranger service, he was big news; all the media collected at his funeral in Dallas.

Gonzaullas was a tender, caring man. He was a great admirer of General Douglas MacArthur, and I can remember watching M. T. cry as the General made his farewell speech to the U. S. Congress and the American public.

M. T. was also a deeply religious man, a strong Presbyterian who served on the board of the Gaston Episcopal Hospital and as chairman of the board for many years.

No one man in law enforcement had any more influence on my entire career as a Ranger than did "Lone Wolf." Someone asked me at his death if I liked the man. I replied without hesitation, "Hell, yes, I liked him—in fact, I loved the man."

If a Ranger has had the good fortune to associate with even one fine leader, he can have no better teacher. To have known three, I consider to be the ultimate honor.

Seven Months To Go

No matter how much a man enjoys working for an outfit, or how long he's been doing it, there comes a time when he starts thinking about hangin' it all up.

For a long lime, I really didn't have it in my mind that one day I would no longer be a Ranger. The word "retirement" to me had always meant a need for planning, so that I could continue to provide for myself and my family. I was told once long ago that the only difference between a man becoming an elderly gentleman or becoming a poor old man is money. I decided early on that I damn sure would rather be the former, and I wasn't going to count on someone else to get me there. I knew that I wouldn't be satisfied with the state employee retirement money, even with Social Security benefits on top of it. It just couldn't provide enough to support me in the manner I wished to live out my "golden years."

About the time I was forty, I started having serious thoughts about how I would get ready for my retirement. Now, the Ranger pay scale has never been what attracted good men to the force. You might say they had better be dedicated lawmen; they surely weren't in it for the money. My first year as a Ranger, I earned

$3,600; my last, $16,000. So it was tough scraping up extra money for investments. Little by little, I managed to put money away, until I had enough to start buying modest rent property and later, stocks and bonds. Thus I was never overly concerned with my financial status come retirement time.

The age at which I would retire, I had always figured to be when I could no longer handle the work as well as I once did. I knew I couldn't tolerate any diminishing of ability that age might bring, and I didn't expect my superiors to, either. There has never been a place in the Rangers for a man to give any less of himself as he grows older than he did at his peak.

Originally, the state retirement age was seventy; I always knew I wouldn't be able to work that long as a Ranger. When the retirement age was reduced to sixty-five, that seemed possible. But gradually, I found myself considering early retirement.

As time went on, I began to see people I had worked with through the years, particularly my superior officers, disappear from the Rangers. Most of them retired; some died. I was saddened by these losses of the company of friends as well as associates. Suddenly I found myself working with men in positions of power, men who were younger than I. I liked them very much, usually; I had no problem respecting younger men, even taking orders from them. I just didn't have the relationship with them that I had with the men I came up with. No matter how much you may like a guy, it is just difficult for a man of sixty to work with a man of thirty-five. The thirty-five-year-old can work longer hours. He sees life differently, with hopes, ambitions, and goals a sixty-year-old can't share, or sometimes, even remember. He's probably as dedicated, maybe even more so, as you were, but you don't feel the spirit of brotherhood you had with your contemporaries. It's nobody's fault, just the way things are.

During my thirty years as a Ranger, I had driven, on the average, 30,000 miles per year on the job. This meant I had logged over a million miles in state cars. Of course, I had to be a little tired of that. The increasing paperwork load was another factor. With the rate of crime surpassing even population increases, and the increasing importance of accurate recordkeeping, I estimate that over the years the paperwork requirement increased five-fold. I found myself more and more irritated at the amount of time I spent on paperwork, time I felt interfered with my every-day duties.

Over the years there had been many changes in methods, regulations, and public opinion. As I grew older and, I guess, set in my ways, I found it hard to accept some of them, even though they may have been right for the times. One regulation I was particularly tired of was the required retraining program. Every two years, each Ranger was sent to Austin for a forty-hour school; I knew it had to be done, I even approved of it in principle, but it got pretty boring going over things I knew by heart and by in-stinct. When I learned in late 1976 that I was due to go to school in 1977, that was the triggering factor to a decision I'd been mull-ing over for months. Finally, in January 1977, I gave my notice of retirement for August 31, 1977, two years earlier than the re-quired.

Many people I knew entered those final few months before retirement with uncertainty and sadness. Not I—I felt prepared for my new life, even anxious, and somewhat relieved to be leav-ing the old one. I felt no qualms over my decision. If I felt any sadness, it was that I had lost people through retirement or death to whom I had been close and with whom I had enjoyed great camaraderie. These included other Rangers, sheriffs and depu-ties, police chiefs and officers, FBI agents, and all kinds of people.

Primarily, upon giving notice I felt a great sense of relax-ation. As each day ended, I came nearer to a time when I wouldn't be subject to twenty-four-hour call; when I wouldn't have to feel that surge of adrenalin that comes from walking into a volatile situation, or the exhaustion that follows it; when I wouldn't have to go pull a body out of a well and start a murder investigation; when I wouldn't have to see the anguish of a mother whose son had killed someone; when I wouldn't have to look at the result of a youthful suicide; when I wouldn't be required to take orders, like them or not. I would be rid of the ever-present media people. I could voice my opinion on issues, when formerly I had to keep mum. I could even enter politics if I desired. In other words, in some ways I felt that finally I would be a full-class citizen.

During all those years of Ranger service, I was never actually afraid for my life. Those last seven months, though, I thought more about getting hurt or killed in the line of duty than I had for the previous thirty years. I suppose I couldn't stand the thought of making it that far and then perhaps losing it all in an instant. So I was careful, very careful. I also didn't wish to pull any blunders that might detract from a successful career. I let someone else take new cases, new leads, and closed the ones I could in the remaining time. I tried very hard to stay out of anything that would result in my having to testify in court later. I began handling all the little details necessary for retirement. I got my paperwork in order. I made application for Social Security benefits. I began getting my equipment together.

Finally, two or three days before my retirement date, I put all my equipment in the state car and drove it to Ranger headquarters in Dallas. I went through all the formalities. As I walked around the office one last time, I kept feeling around for something in my pocket. Finally I realized it was the car keys which had always been there, which I had already turned in. I asked the sheriff to give me a ride home.

The final step was the small luncheon held on the first of September, with all the Rangers, the secretary, and four or five retirees. "You've done a great job and we'll not forget you," they all said. It was nice to hear all those kind things, but I'd heard them before, at retirement functions for others before me, and I knew that it just doesn't work out that way. I had to lay it down then, to walk away from it, and to start my new life.

I have no regrets and a great many good things to remember. No job is perfect, but this one was always interesting and frequently rewarding, and not everyone can say that about a chosen career. If I had it to do all over again, I would gladly and proudly serve as a Texas Ranger once more. But if someone came to me and told me I could be a Ranger again *now,* at any salary and at any location, I would quickly say no, I have had my time. I am done.

To gauge his progress in life, a man must be able to look at the past, at where he has been. I am proud to have been a member of Texas' oldest and most respected law enforcement agency.

Sometimes now, when I attend Ranger functions and see those serving our state, they look awfully young to me, maybe because I sometimes feel awfully old in their presence. Some of them were in diapers while I was out there working six counties. Now they dress just a little differently from the way we did— styles do change, and Western wear is "in." And they drive air-conditioned cars hooked up to electronic data systems smarter than all of us. A lot of them have degrees now. I don't resent their right to carry on the traditions of the Rangers in the way they see fit. It feels good to let them handle it. But in a way, I feel sorry for the young ones. They only have the future. I have the past.

☆ Afterword

Erik Rigler

It is at family gatherings that I like to watch my father. Surrounded by five daughters, three sons and eighteen grandchildren, he is in his element. His children have done well: teachers, an accountant, a computer engineer, salespersons, secretaries and homemakers. The varied interests of his offspring are a credit to the man, as he supported each child and grandchild in their respective career choices. I was the only one to follow in his footsteps and go into law enforcement.

My first recollection of my father as a Texas Ranger comes from a time when I was about five years old. My room in our old two-story home on Gainesville's tree-lined Lindsay Street was immediately above his bedroom, and it was late into the night when I heard the phone ring and listened drowsily to his one-sided conversation. Moments later, I heard his car start and leave the driveway as he answered an emergency call.

Still later that night, I was awakened again by my father returning to our house with two small, frightened boys. My dad rounded up pajamas for the boys and saw that they had a place to sleep. One of the boys, about my age, was put into an extra bed in my room. Through the boy's sobs, he spilled out his story, and I learned that there had been a family disturbance. His father had gone berserk and had pointed a shotgun at the boys, threatening to kill both of them. My father had stepped between the boys and their father, risking his life to take the gun from the man. I was intrigued by the incident and very proud of my father. Within a few days of that incident, my dad announced that there was a meeting of his Ranger company at the ranch of Tom Hickman, a former Texas Ranger captain, and he wanted me to go with him. It was quite an honor: only the best-behaved children of Texas Rangers got to go to social gatherings with their fathers.

The setting was like one from the movie "Giant." The Hickman place was a hard-scrabble ranch south of Gainesville. The event was attended by several dozen Rangers and an equal number of ranchers, bankers, doctors and other assorted businessmen, all wearing boots and Western attire.

A long trench had been dug into the rocky ground and filled with red-hot mesquite wood. Over this stood grills holding a large assortment of sizzling beef. A few other children were there, but I stuck close to my father; I wanted to see and hear the other Rangers speak to him and, more important, hear him tell the story of how he stepped in front of a loaded shotgun to protect the two small boys.

Over the course of the afternoon I observed my father participate in numerous conversations with the Rangers and guests but, strangely, not one person brought up the topic of his brave act. I wanted to burst into the conversations and ensure that each person there knew about the incident; but I could not do so, because I knew that as a special junior guest, I had no status in the conversation.

Still, as the afternoon shadows grew longer, I saw my father as the center of many conversations, telling first a story about a notorious burglar and then a humorous tale about an old sheriff he knew. Then, as the gathering was ending, I saw all of the Rangers, one by one, stop by to shake my father's hand prior to leaving for their respective offices; it was then I knew that they were well aware of his act of bravery. It was a topic that was not discussed among these men.

That was the moment when I first knew that I wanted to be like him, to work in law enforcement and to have the respect of my peers.

While in college, I worked first for a sheriff's department and then for a police department. My law enforcement career after college was delayed while I served as a Navy pilot during the Vietnam War. Prior to leaving the service, I decided to work on a Master's degree in criminal justice. Two Special Agents who were in one of my classes recruited me into the Federal Bureau of Investigation when my degree was completed.

I had assignments in Washington, D.C.; Omaha, Nebraska; South Bend, Indiana; and McAllen and San Antonio, Texas. After a twenty-two-year career, I retired from the FBI and once again followed in my father's footsteps, this time into a job with a state law enforcement agency.

At a recent family reunion on the occasion of my father's 80th birthday, I spoke with him regarding our careers and some of the similar events they contained.

While I was working for the police department in Denton— trying to learn enough German to pass one last course and get my undergraduate degree—I was contacted by an officer of the Dallas Police Department to help his unit assess the threat to President John F. Kennedy prior to his ill-fated trip to Texas. The Dallas officer wanted me to visit the Turtle Creek Boulevard residence of former U.S. Army General Edwin A. Walker.

Walker, who had resigned his commission over a dispute with his senior officers related to his conduct in Germany, had become an outspoken political critic. The Dallas Police Department felt that Walker was among a number of potential threats the president would face. I was asked to visit the general as a college student and develop any information that would indicate Walker was planning to use violence to protest the president's visit.

I visited with the general on Turtle Creek and subsequently told the police officers in Dallas that General Walker spoke only of minor peaceful protests. On the second of these visits, in that fateful month of November 1963, the general, seated in a leather reclining chair, pointed to a bullet hole in the wall above his head, fired by someone from outside his home. Later we would learn that the bullet was fired by a man named Lee Harvey Oswald, President Kennedy's assassin and the future target of Jack Ruby.

I recall speaking briefly with my father on the morning of the presidential visit, telling him of my time at General Walker's house and of my findings. He told me that he and fifty of his fellow Texas Rangers were assigned to the protection detail at Market Hall on Dallas' Stemmons Expressway. On the day of the visit he and his associates, all with freshly shined boots and new Stetson hats, waited for a president who never arrived. When he learned the awful news, my father said he knew that this country would never be the same. I later learned that he spent time working at the Dallas County Sheriff's Department on that day and was present when Oswald was brought in for questioning.

During the last years of his law enforcement career and the first of mine, I frequently called him for advice. While working on the 1979 assassination of U.S. District Court Judge John H. Wood of San Antonio, I sought his advice when the case had hit rock bottom and it seemed as if we would never solve the mystery of the judge's murder. "Patience" was his one-word suggestion. I asked for more and he said, "The breaks will come when they are ready. Just protect your evidence and be patient." He was right.

When a suspected shooter in the case was identified as

Charles Voyde Harrelson, I called my father to tell him about it. "Yes," he said, "I know of Harrelson; I have interviewed him on occasion. He used to carry a business card with 'Murder for Hire' on it, but no one really believed him. You have the right man."

It was my father's .38 caliber Smith & Wesson revolver, Serial Number 42000, that I carried for two decades after he had laid it down. Neither of us ever fired it in a hostile situation, only on training days. I carried his Texas Ranger business card behind my FBI credentials for twenty-two years.

It was my father's ability to make friends anywhere that I envied most. As a kid growing up in Gainesville, I frequently saw him place an offender in jail and then, after a few days, talk the judge into releasing him. He would find the man a job and a home for his family and treat him with respect. He would work late to counsel the errant child of frantic parents and steer the youth away from life as a criminal, then return home to lead his sons in a game of frontyard baseball or football, or the inevitable: cleaning house. "Let's smug-up the place," he would say. My brothers and I would groan.

His case involving the 1948 disappearance of young Virginia Carpenter from a Denton campus was strangely paralleled by my 1980s case involving the disappearance of Kim Leggett, a twenty-two-year-old wife and mother from Mercedes, Texas. And my case, like his, is still pending after years with no witness, no body, no strong suspect or subject, and no solution in sight. We both find these cases difficult to talk about, as they did not end well. Most people want a solution to a kidnapping in fifty minutes with three commercials, just like on the television programs, but it doesn't always happen that way.

As I travel, I still find myself looking for Kim in airports, stores and restaurants. I think she is still alive, as I know my father thought Carpenter was. My dad confesses that he has also looked for Virginia wherever he goes. Together we wonder what more we could have given to the investigations that might have brought the victims back.

Although he's known some tough times, my dad has never lost his sense of humor. Upon the occasion of my completing the FBI's New Agent Training in Quantico, Virginia, he sent me a brief note that provided a valuable tip to a newly designated law enforcement officer:

"Never marry a blonde, never buy a house with a flat root and never pick up a piece of evidence that won't fit in an envelope." The last was a bit of dry humor related to a police detective we both knew, who gathered so much evidence that he found it difficult to store and impossible to dispose of long after the case was closed.

And so it is, in the autumn of his life, that I admire my father the most. Surrounded by his wife, sons, daughters and grandchildren, he is content. (It also helps that he still works five days a week as an investment counselor and co-owner of a bail-bond business.) I see him tease granddaughters Gina and Natalie. They play a game called "Love You, Gotcha!" in which the winner is the first to call out the phrase. He is a lucky man, and I am lucky to have him as my father.

Erik and Lewis Rigler holding Erik's retirement plaque from the
Federal Bureau of Investigation.

INDEX